MW01065887

Paul Hoer's

Slices

of East Audrain

Finding histories PEH Solving mysteries

Celebrating 175 Years of Audrain History

History

Slices of East Audrain History
Copyright © 2009
Paul Hoer

The Scribe's Closet Publications
702 South Missouri
Macon, MO 63552
www.thescribesclosetpublications.com

All rights reserved.
This book may not be reproduced in whole or in part
or transmitted in any form without written permission
from the publisher, except by a reviewer
who may quote a brief passage in a review:
nor may any part of the book be reproduced,
stored in a retrieval system, or transmitted in any form
or by any means, electronic, mechanical, photocopied,
recorded, or other without written permission
from the publisher.

First Printing, 2011

ISBN 978-0-9832570-1-1

Printed in The United States of America

Cover and Chapter Art by Vickie Welschmeyer Robinson

Preface

In this one hundred and seventy-fifth year since the founding of Audrain County, much has transpired within its borders. This book focuses on the eastern part of the county, presenting slices of historical events and places with varying degrees of importance. It is an attempt to preserve the past and offer it to the reader in an enjoyable way. Some of the stories were discovered by the writer and expanded upon through research. Others were built from people's suggestions and conversations.

There is a strong hint of genealogy mixed in with the history. The writer had an interest in revealing what happened to the characters after an event took place. This was the purpose in extending the stories. The endnotes were added to give those interested in further research a starting point, whether it be toward genealogy or history.

The author offers his thanks to those at the Audrain County Area Genealogical Library and the Mexico-Audrain County Library, who helped and supported this undertaking. A special thank you goes to Cricket Russom for her research help, and to Vickie Welschmeyer Robinson for her interesting and appropriate artwork.

Paul Hoer, July, 2011

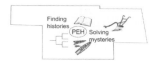

Missouri State Gazeteer and Business Directory, 1876 – 1877
R. L. Polk and Co., Publishers
Found at the Missouri State Historical Society, Columbia, MO

Martinsburgh

A village on the St. Louis, Kansas City and Northern (?) Railway in Audrain County, 14 miles east of Mexico, the county seat, and 94 miles northwest of St. Louis; it was settled in 1859 and incorporated in 1871; population 400; mail daily Leroy Wilson, postmaster.

Business Directory

Brown,	....	Miller
Carver, B. E.	....	Carriage Maker
Clark, C. B.	....	Hotel Proprietor
Clifton, H. T.	....	Blacksmith
Dodson, S. M.	....	Physician
Douglass, E. R.	....	Physician
Fish, T. R.	....	Machine Agent
Garrett, P. H.	....	General Store
Howard, D. C.	....	Express& Station Agent
Lowden, T. J.	....	Broom Manufacturer
Marlow, Rev. T. J.	....	
Martin, William H.	....	Lawyer
Martin & Fike	....	Millinery
Muster, J. S.	....	Lumber
Owen, D. T.	....	Blacksmith
Rogers, M. & C.	....	Millinery
Stephenson, J. P.	....	Hardware
Tapscott, A. W.	....	Lumber
Torryson, J. R.	....	Blacksmith
Vandevanter, A. M.	....	Physician
Weatherford, J. T. & Co.	....	Druggist
Weatherford & Alloway	....	General Store
Wilson, Leroy	....	Grocer

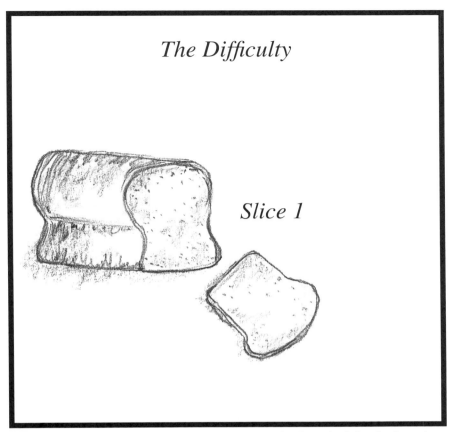

The Difficulty

Slice 1

In 1871, a wild-west style shooting took place in Martinsburgh, Audrain County, Missouri. It's a tale of how three men's lives came together on a summer evening, and with a variety of firearms, produced a tragedy. When under the scrutiny of the law, those who witnessed the shooting and the events leading to it always referred to them as *The Difficulty*.

Martinsburgh, ending with an h, was the spelling of the town name at the time. In 1890 President Harrison created the U. S. Board of Geographic Names. A pronouncement by this Board stated that post office names ending in "burgh" should drop the final "h," Thus, Martinsburgh became Martinsburg.

Milton P. Scott and Samuel W. Crutcher were both born in Monroe County, Missouri. Sam was born in 1843 and Milton in 1847. As a very young man, Sam chose to defend the Confederate States of America in the War Between the States. He joined the 11th Missouri Infantry under the command of Colonel Simon P. Burns. This unit served in Parson's and Burn's Brigade, Trans-Mississippi Department, and fought in Arkansas and Louisiana.

5

Sam was a private in Company K.[1]

He was a tinner by trade and had a shop on Washington Street in Martinsburgh. Sam had an interest in Thadeus Hanes' saddler's shop. This shop was an addition on the back of the tin shop.

Sam's father was Ambrose Crutcher, a Monroe County pioneer, born in Kentucky. He later moved to Pike County, Missouri, where he married, and finally settled in Monroe County in 1831. He was a farmer and master blacksmith in Paris, Missouri.[2]

Milton's father was Davis Scott. As a pioneer, he worked his way to Monroe County from Kentucky and became a farmer. Both Ambrose and Davis had large families and were long lived. Ambrose had been a slaveholder.

Although Sam and Milton probably knew each other in Monroe County, there in no available evidence that the beginning of The Difficulty took place there. Instead it seems much more likely that the problems began in Martinsburgh between Milton Scott and Augustus W. Tapscott. Augustus and his wife Sally, were Virginians who had moved west in 1854, eventually settling in Martinsburgh. They raised two daughters: Emma P. and Clara W., called Katie.

Augustus Tapscott was often referred to as Captain Tapscott. As a young man in Virginia he commanded a company of state militia. It was a sharp outfit, well drilled, and Augustus appears to have been proud of that fact. His title stuck. Mr. Tapscott was also Justice of the Peace, an officer of the county court. His service to the county was not continuous, he having served before and after The Difficulty. By 1884 he had spent eighteen years as a Justice of the Peace for Audrain County.[3]

As with many of the early pioneers, the Captain was involved in numerous businesses. He was a farmer and shopkeeper. One year he spent as postmaster of the Loutre Post Office just prior to the Civil War, better known in Martinsburgh by its southern appellation, the War Between the States.[4] The Loutre Post Office was developed from the Shy Post Office and eventually became the Martinsburgh Post Office. In 1871 Capt. Tapscott was a lumber dealer in Martinsburgh.[5]

No doubt one reason Milton visited Martinsburgh in the first place was to see his sister, Sarah Crigler. John Crigler, Sarah's husband, came to Martinsburgh from Monroe County after his first wife, Elizabeth, had died and he married Sarah F. Scott, Milton's older sister. John Crigler was responsible for Martinsburgh's easterly growth in 1866 with the Crigler Addition to Martinsburgh.

It is apparent that Milton Scott was interested in Katie Tapscott. John lived next door to Augustus Tapscott, putting Milton in close proximity to his desire, sixteen-year-old Katie. This also brought him into conflict with Capt. Tapscott, who had forbidden him to

6

enter the house.

Mrs. Elizabeth Hall, wife of preacher Alfred Hall, provides insight into the relationship of Milton Scott and Katie Tapscott. In testimony she gave in court, she spoke of being "present in this house at preaching one night. Mr. Tapscott and Mr. Scott were both here. I do not remember where Mr. Tapscott and Mr. Scott sat that night. Mr. Scott and Miss Katie Tapscott started out of the house together. I don't know how much further they went [as] I did not see them on the road home."[6]

Mrs. Hall explained that the last time Mr. Scott was in Martinsburgh was six months or maybe more before he was killed. She stated, "I was at Mr. Tapscott's the morning Milton Scott left Martinsburgh. Scott came into the room where myself and daughter were sitting at Mr. Tapscott's and took a seat. He asked where Katie was. I told him she was in the other room. While I was telling him, she got up and came into the room where he was."

"Katie and him had a chat of about half an hour,"[7] Mrs. Hall continued. "They set a few minutes on the side of the bed and he started to go away and they went into the hall. When he left he saw the train coming and went to the depot."[8]

Mrs. Hall claimed to have told Milton when he came in on that occasion that he had better go away and stay away for a while. She informed him of the fact that "they are sort of down on you in this town."[9] She said that she didn't know that Milton had been forbidden to come into the house until after he was gone.

When Mr. Tapscott was speaking in court on his own behalf, the first thing he mentioned was banning Milton Scott. He said, "Mr. Scott visited my house several times up to last spring. I had a conversation with Mr. Scott. I told him I did not want him to visit my family. He seemed to become enraged. I told him I had a right to forbid his coming there."[10]

The next day Scott stopped by Tapscott's lumber shed. He remarked, "that I am as good as any other damned man."[11] Augustus told him he did not want to discuss his character.

In another portion of his statement, Mr. Tapscott again touched on the subject. "I think Scott had been visiting my family twelve months, more or less, before I prohibited him from visiting my family, myself, wife, and children. I presume in visiting my family that his object was to visit my daughter. I was fearful that my daughter and Mr. Scott were engaged, though she denied it to me through my wife."[11]

"My reasons for objecting to his visiting my family was on account of reports I had heard of his conduct. At the time I forbid his visiting my family further, which was last spring, my daughter was about sixteen and a half years old. He came to my house once afterwards, as well as I can remember, without my permission."[12]

Sam Crutcher was drawn into this mix in a most bizarre and sad way. While The Difficulty between Milton and Augustus was developing, Samuel Crutcher married Emma Tapscott on the 29th day of December, 1870. He became a part of the Tapscott family. He moved out of his boarding room with John Stephens, a blacksmith, and into the Tapscott household.

Eleven days later on January eighth, Emma died. It stated in the 1884 History of Audrain County that she died "before the flowers had faded on her wedding wreath."[13] The cause of her death is unknown but there were plenty of diseases waiting to carry an individual off in 1871.[14]

Emma was buried in the Old Village Cemetery in Mexico, Audrain County, Missouri. Her gravestone, although broken by vandals, is still legible in the north wall at the cemetery. It is a lovely stone with the hand of God reaching from a cloud to pluck a rose from earth. Emma was nineteen years, eight months, and six days old. Sam continued to maintain a sleeping room in the Tapscott home.

Emma's Tombstone, Old Village Cemetery, Mexico, MO

In the months that Milton Scott was away from Martinsburgh he brooded about the turn of events. The deep negative feelings he later displays toward Capt. Tapscott and Sam Crutcher must have

8

incubated in his mind for some time before he brought them to Martinsburgh with a plan of action. He chafed at the idea, real or imagined, that Sam was vying with him for the affections of Katie Tapscott.

There is convincing evidence that Milton visited Martinsburgh at least once and maybe twice in the months before August first. There are some small clues that he was moving up and down the North Missouri Railroad traveling as far to the east as St. Louis. It would have been easy to step off the train at Martinsburgh.

According to Robert Farthing, a cooper in Martinsburg, Milton had been in the depot in May or June because he had talked to him there. He reported that Sam had come up and asked Milton where Jameson, a future Martinsburg businessman, was. "What's the matter, Milton?"[15] The remainder of that page is missing and we are left in the dark as to his reply. This indicates, however, that at that time Sam had already been drawn into The Difficulty.

Robert Armstrong, one of Martinsburg's blacksmiths, reported on that conversation in the depot. He repeated, "that Scott said he did not want to have anything to do with any such a damned two-faced man as he (Crutcher) was."[16]

It is certain that Milton Scott arrived in Martinsburg on the last day of July. David Rice, who ran an eatinghouse, testified that Milton had come in that evening. He stated, "He came on the train. Went below and returned before sundown. He came into my house, shook hands with me and talked some time."[17] The phrase "went below" at that time meant that he had come from the west (Mexico), had passed Martinsburg and had gone east to Wellsville, Montgomery City, or wherever and had then come back to Martinsburg before dark.[18]

While Milton was eating supper and visiting with Mr. Rice, Sam attended his lodge meeting, the A F and A M (Ancient, Free, and Accepted Masons). He stayed until ten p.m. and then returned to his shop. He went to the front door to go across the street to Mr. French's store, but saw that the store was closed. He saw a light in Fike and Dillard's Saloon across the street and heard considerable talking. Milton Scott was there.

Sam heard Robert Armstrong ask Milton to stay the night with him. Milton refused and eventually started off with his young nephew, Walter Crigler. When they passed Sam, one of them said, "There is Crutcher now."[19]

Sixty yards down the street the two argued. Walter went on home and Milton returned up the street heading for Sam, who stepped back into his shop and nearly closed the door. Milton changed direction and went back to the saloon. Sam Crutcher went to bed.

As the new day of August 1st, 1871 began, the workers of Martinsburgh settled into their tasks for the day. Milton Scott moved through the town's shops and left a trail of bitterness. What is strange is that he did this in a playful, carefree way. He sat on the counter in the grocery and chatted with acquaintances. He seemed to some people to be happy-go-lucky. If the talk turned, however, to why he was in town or about Capt. Tapscott or Sam Crutcher, it was a different story.

Charles B. Clark, the Marshal of the town, testified that Mr. Scott had said to him "that if Crutcher gave him a chance, God damned him, he would shoot his guts out."[20] He also commented to Marshal Clark about Tapscott. He (Scott) called him a "God damned old lying s___a__, he has lied upon me and disgraced me."[21] The writer thought the Marshal would have been more forceful in dealing with Mr. Scott.

Instead, Clark's only admonition to Milton Scott was, "Says I, Milton, my son, says I, you lay yourself liable to be shot down just like a dog in the street, says I.[22] They can have you bound over to appeals."[23]

Marshal Clark did not tell anyone of this conversation and admitted, "I took no steps toward arresting the deceased."[24] In fact, Marshal Charles Clark went home.

In the morning of that day, Frank Dillard found Milton Scott in the back room of the store. He was revolving the cylinder of his pistol. When asked what he was doing he said he had some empty cartridges and wanted to reload it. He thought he might have a row with Crutcher that day.

Daniel Brooks swore he saw Milton Scott in Fike's Grocery leaning against the counter loading a revolver. He heard him say "that he intended to kill Sam Crutcher before he left town."[25]

Everywhere Scott went, he left a message of the coming showdown with Crutcher and Tapscott. He went into Thadeus Hanes' saddler's shop and told Thad "he had had a Difficulty with Mr. Crutcher and had come to Martinsburgh to settle it."[26] Milton wanted Thad to deliver a message to Sam to come out into the street and exchange shots with him. He said, "he did not want to shoot him down like a coward or a dog but wanted him to come and fight like a man."[27] Once he said he would give Sam the first shot.

Thad delivered the message to Sam and Sam passed it to Capt. Tapscott. They decided to meet with W. H. Martin, a lawyer and son of the founder of Martinsburgh. Sam, Augustus, Thad, and William Martin met in Sam's bedroom at Tapscott's house. Sam and Augustus sought advice on what they should do in the face of the impending threat.

10

William Martin had earlier heard Scott curse Capt. Tapscott and was aware of the bad feeling between Crutcher and Tapscott on the one part and Milton Scott on the other. He also had seen Scott mock Tapscott on the platform in front of Gantt's Store. He advised them "to avoid Scott during that evening particularily, and in fact during his stay in Martinsburgh."[28] He didn't think they were safe in Scott's presence. They should keep an eye on Scott, be on the defensive, and if Scott made an overt move, defend themselves. He told them to arm themselves, but not to become aggressors.

Mr. Hanes, who was the Constable of Loutre Township,[29] delivered the message to Scott. Milton was upset with the answer Thad gave him. Scott said "that it would not do. That he had come here for the purpose of settling this Difficulty by killing Sam or Sam killing him."[30] He then roundly cursed Sam. "He called Sam a damned cowardly son of a bitch. Then he immediately took it back and said, 'Thad, I take that back. I call no man a son of a bitch.' He then called him a damned cowardly puppy."[31] He also said that if he did not get him that day, he would get him sometime.

Sam asked Thad to get him a horse. He rode the horse south of town three quarters of a mile to the home of Thomas Garrard, the banker, who lived in the old William R. Martin house. Only Mrs. Garrard was home. Sam borrowed a double-barreled shotgun. When he got the gun he said, "ask me no questions and I'll tell you nothing."[32] He quickly rode back to town. Sam loaded the shotgun, putting nine to twelve buckshot in each barrel.

Capt. Tapscott had also had his share of abuse from Milton Scott. Scott usually cursed him every time he saw him. Once when they went to preaching in a house Scott came in and sat next to him near the pulpit. Scott crossed his legs and kicked Capt. Tapscott four or five times in the ankle joint. Others heard the abuse that was heaped upon Tapscott and testified to it in court. The Captain did not have a weapon, but was able to secure one, a pepperbox revolver.

H. H. Washburn said he had eaten lunch with Scott and saw no pistol on him. He was also in the grocery store with Scott ten minutes before The Difficulty progressed, and said Milton did not seem to be under the influence of liquor. Five minutes before the shooting, Milton bought a cigar from Frank Dillard and lit it up.

Capt. Tapscott and several others were in the alley between Gantt's Store and Dr. Tucker's office, pitching quoits.[33] Thad Hanes came and whispered in Capt. Tapscott's ear. Then he excused himself and left. He went to the tin shop and someone saw him later in Dodson's Drugstore.

As Scott left the store puffing his cigar, he told Frank Dillard that he was going to walk by Crutcher's and see if he would speak to him. "If he does," said Scott, "I'll bust him at the time."[34] Those were his last words.

Sam Crutcher finished loading the shotgun and put it in the shop. He had avoided going to the front door for a couple of hours, but now went to see what was happening. When Sam saw Milton advancing toward him from Fike and Dillard's across the street, he must have felt it was time to act.

He stepped back into the shop and reappeared with the shotgun. Scott continued toward Crutcher with his hand on his hip. Crutcher allowed time for people to get out of the way. Then Crutcher lowered the gun and fired.

Milton slapped his thigh in reaction, at the same time pulling a revolver from behind his back and fired. At almost the same moment, Crutcher fired again. Witnesses said Scott was dressed in black, and when Crutcher fired Milton's coattail flew up. Another witness said he saw the dust fly from Milton's clothes.

When Milton fired at Crutcher, he began to run toward him. Crutcher stepped back into the building, put down the shotgun, and reappeared with a large revolver. They both fired nearly together. Crutcher's cylinder on his pistol would not revolve, so he jumped back into the shop and slammed the door. He was wounded. Scott was running up on the platform, and upon reaching the door he was knocked back a little by it being slammed. Milton, confronted by the closed-door, put his pistol against it and fired.

In Dr. Dodson's Drug Store next door, Capt. Tapscott, who had been sitting in a chair, rose and fired out the door. Milton was moving sideways from Crutcher's shop to the front of the drug-store. He fired at Tapscott, putting a ball through the east shutter and into the ceiling. He looked back over his right shoulder at Crutcher's tin shop. Tapscott fired again with some effect. Scott threw up his arm and fired. He then quickly whirled around and started for Gantt's Store. Witnesses variously described Scott's retreat to Gantt's Store as a walk, a run, a double-quick, or a stagger.

Thomas Preston, a storekeeper, who had been in the alley pitching quoits, stepped around Dr. Tucker's office to observe once the shooting began. When Scott began to go in the direction of Gantt's Store, Preston saw Tapscott present his pistol in his direction. Preston stepped behind the office. He heard the report of Tapscott's third shot. Thomas Preston was standing still when Scott came by the end of the alley. Preston stated, "I saw blood on his shirt bosom. As he got near the platform of Gantt's Store, he spit out a mouthful of blood."[35]

Preston followed Scott onto the platform. Through the side-lights of the door he was able to see Scott falling. Milton's hand touched the counter and he fell. Preston continued, "I ran to him

12

and turned him over. He had his pistol in his right hand and the stump of a cigar between the fingers of his left hand."[36] The pistol was handed to P. H. Gantt, the store's owner. He inspected it and found it was cocked with one cartridge left. Scott had fired five shots.

Captain Tapscott came across the street to see how badly Milton was hurt. A crowd had gathered around Scott in the store. When Tapscott heard Scott was dead, he said, "Oh," and left.

David Owen came up the street from his blacksmith shop, west on Washington Street, after seeing the end of the shooting. He went to see where Crutcher was. Sam was wounded, but David didn't go in to him as they were carrying him off. As he was carried to Capt. Tapscott's house, Mr. Crutcher remarked, "that he had told the Captain that he did not want him to have anything to do with it."[37]

Sam Crutcher had fired both barrels of the shotgun and once with his revolver. He hit Milton Scott with all three shots. We can assume that the revolver was one Sam had carried during his Civil War days and obviously was not in good repair.

Milton fired three times at Sam. The first ball hit three feet east of the door. The second one hit Sam "in the breast near the left nipple."[38] His third shot hit the door. Milton fired two times at Capt. Tapscott in the drug store. One shot went through the shutter and into the ceiling. The other shot could not be found.

Tapscott fired three shots at Milton. Tapscott's first shot seems to have missed. His second shot at close range hit Scott. The third shot fired as Scott departed the scene remains a mystery. It obviously was a miss.

Dr. M. M. Tucker inspected Scott's wounds that evening of August first. Milton had been hit with twelve buckshot, the doctor noted, "one shot in the left leg below the knee, five shots in the left leg above the knee. Six shots in the right leg above the knee." It appears that Sam was following his training as a soldier. Soldiers were told to aim low so they wouldn't overshoot the enemy.

Dr. Tucker observed two wounds in the breast that he considered to be the cause of death. The lower wound was the larger one and the writer assumes it was caused by Crutcher's larger caliber pistol. It was described as "one shot on the third rib on the right side near the sternum passing below the rib entering the lungs ranging inward and downward."[40] The upper wound being smaller was more likely to have been caused by Tapscott's smaller caliber pistol. "One [shot] in the right clavicle near the sternal articulation ranging below the clavicle entering the lung ranging inward and downward."[41]

The week following the shooting was quiet. Sam Crutcher began to heal. Milton Scott was laid to rest three quarters of a mile south of Martinsburgh on John Crigler's land in what is now called the Old Martinsburg Cemetery.

On the 8th of August, Thomas Scott, Milton's brother, came to Mexico from Paris seeking the arrest of Crutcher and Tapscott for murder. He swore an affidavit before Enoch Hooten, Justice of the Peace for Audrain County. Justice Hooten wrote out an arrest warrant that same day.

W. H. White, Sheriff of Audrain County, executed the writ and arrested Crutcher and Tapscott on the 9th of August. They were brought before Justices of the Peace Enoch Hooten and George B. Leachman. The court found probable cause that an offense had been committed. A one thousand dollar recognizance was required of each defendant and they were discharged.[42]

Justices Leachman and Hooten recalled Crutcher and Tapscott on the 15th of August. They were to appear at the October term of the court and their recognizance was raised to two thousand dollars each.[43]

Several circuit court documents are obviously missing. For example, a report of the October term session is unavailable. It is known, however, that this session was held in the public schoolhouse at Martinsburgh. It had to have ended in a continuance or a referral to a grand jury.

The June term 1872 was a meeting of the grand jury. They sat for eight days and swore twenty witnesses. Seventy-five pieces of evidence were investigated. Circuit Attorney C. E. Peers[44] seems to have put more blame on Tapscott.

A badly damaged and partial document written by Justice Hooten mentioned that seventy-five pieces of evidence were recorded in writing and signed by the witnesses. It stated, "All papers were attached together with all entries."[45]

Sadly these documents did not survive and the evidential list is lost. A list of fees did survive and it shows the witnesses who were present. It also presented the costs incurred by the court.[46]

At this juncture all documentation ends. Conclusions beyond this point had to be based on assumptions. Tapscott and Crutcher went on with their lives. From this we must assume the grand jury either dismissed the case as self-defense or they referred the case for trial. If the latter situation were true, we can further reason that the pair had been found not guilty.

Captain Tapscott regained his position of Justice of the Peace for Audrain County. This seems certain proof of his vindication.

We can conclude the story of The Difficulty here. The writer has added an epilogue to include some additional information about a few of the characters and their lives beyond The Difficulty.

14

Epilogue

Samuel W. Crutcher married the Tapscott's younger daughter, Katie, on the 15th of October in 1873. Was he competing with Milton Scott for Katie's affection? If so, he waited a suitable period of time. They lived on lots 7 and 8, Block 1, Crigler's Addition in Martinsburg. This is the present location of the St. Joseph School building. In 1876 a son was born to them. His name was Thomas E. Crutcher. Katie seems to have been living in Monroe County. This is verified by Tom Crutcher's obituary, which reports he was born in Monroe County.

Tragedy again came to Sam and Augustus. Only the barest of inferences indicated Katie's passing after a few years of marriage. She died 17 Feb 1876 and was buried in Crutcher's Cemetery, north of Stoutsville, Monroe County, MO.[47] It seems probable that she died in childbirth. There is a conflict with T. E.'s birthdate. This is not an unusual occurrence. Katie's death brought obvious change to Sam's life. At some point Sam decided to remove to Texas.

Texas was becoming a magnet for settlers in the 1870's.[48] William H. Martin, who gave Sam legal advice, departed Martinsburgh for Brownwood, Texas in 1876. The 1880 Census shows him as a drug dealer.[49] He later became a banker, had a newspaper, and prospered.

George B. Leachman, Justice of the Peace for Loutre Township during The Difficulty, also went to Texas. He settled in Dallas and he and his son, George Jr., became agents for a sewing machine company. The younger George eventually bought a laundry. He was successful and he continued acquiring laundries until he owned all the laundries in Dallas. He was another Martinsburgh success story.[50]

Sam also went to Texas. This may be an indication of the disruption in his life. By 1879 Sam was divesting himself of some of his Martinsburgh property. He sold eighty acres of farmland to Hubert Fennewald in August of that year. The western end of this eighty was where the Fennewald School was later located. When that sale was made Sam was in Tarrant County, Texas. Tarrant County is the area of the present Fort Worth.

Thomas Crutcher was enumerated twice in the 1880 U. S. Census. He was counted in Martinsburgh with his Grandparents, the Tapscotts, and again in Monroe County with the Crutcher Grandparents. Thomas did not move to Texas with his father. He was raised in Monroe County, MO. Sam had become a traveling merchant by then. He began working out of Abilene and sold hardware and farm implements to frontier posts over the surrounding area of pioneer Texas. At census time he was rooming in Abilene, Taylor County, Texas. He eventually settled in Nolan County next door at Sweetwater, Texas, around 1884. After Sam settled in Texas, his life blossomed once again in Sweetwater. Sam met and married a widow, Della Houser Pearce, in Abilene, Taylor County, Texas. They were married on 7 February 1884. Della had four children by her marriage to William Pearce. Three lived to adulthood. Sam and Della had three additional children; Ella, Estelle, and Charles W. Crutcher.[51]

Capt. Tapscott continued his lumber business until 1884. It was then taken over by David Owen, a former blacksmith in Martinsburgh and also a witness to The Difficulty. David Turner Owen was murdered in St. Louis in 1910, apparently by his son, Turner. The case against his son was dropped for lack of evidence.

Death took Sally Tapscott on the 24th of April in 1882. Augustus and his wife were long time members of the Christian Church in Martinsburgh. The Captain was for many years the secretary of the Masonic Lodge there.

As Justice of the Peace for Loutre Township, Augustus Tapscott had several duties. One such duty was to publish or have published reports of strays. Strays were farm animals that had disappeared for one reason or another. One of the Captain's stray reports was in the Mexico Weekly Ledger in November of 1876.[53]

Another duty of the Justice was to perform weddings, reports of which were also published. Squire (a name sometimes given to county officials) Tapscott married Miss Eliza Nichols and John Howard, four miles north of Martinsburgh, on 7 March 1883, according to the Weekly Ledger.[54] This farm is still in the Nichols possession. It is now owned by Orville Nichols and is a Century Farm plus.

Augustus sold his town property in the mid 1880's and then disappears from history. His Martinsburgh home was razed in 1925. Frank Jacobi's home replaced the Tapscott house. It is not known when A. W. Tapscott died or where he and his wife are buried. Liberty Cemetery in Callaway County is the most likely location as many of the Christians of Martinsburgh are buried there. There are no stones to verify it. Maybe since their girls were deceased there was no one left to mark their graves. Capt. Tapscott's life at its end is a mystery. The writer continues to seek these elusive answers.

As was stated, Thomas Elliot Crutcher grew up in Monroe County. He left Monroe County in 1894 at age 18 to join his father in business in Sweetwater, Nolan County, Texas. He became a soldier in 1898 and fought in the Spanish-American War. Upon discharge he returned to Nolan County.

Tom served Nolan County in various capacities for many years.

16

In 1903 he married Lona Hopkins, a daughter of Nolan County pioneers. In 1904 he served as sheriff and tax collector. He spent six years as sheriff and ten years as tax collector.

T. E. superintended various public works including the water department. His last seven years were spent as office manager for the sheriff. He and Lona had two children, Sam and Mary. Mary became a member of the editorial staff of a newspaper, the Fort Worth Press.[55] She never married.

Tom and his family are buried in Sweetwater. A medallion on his grave reflects his service in the Spanish-American War.

On the second of June 1895, the St. Louis Republic listed on page 19 the names of Missourians who attended the 1895 Reunion of Confederate Soldiers in Houston, Texas. S. W. Crutcher is shown from Sweetwater, Texas and a veteran of the Eleventh Missouri Infantry, Burn's Brigade.

Sam was obviously proud of his efforts on behalf of the Confederate cause. His grave is marked with a stone and two cast medallions. One is the Confederate marker, Deo Vindice (God will vindicate us), and the other is the B.P.O.E. (Elks) marker.

Sam's C. S. A. Marker, City Cemetery, Sweetwater, Texas.
Courtesy Janie Healer Davis, Sweetwater.

Samuel had several businesses during his life in Texas. For some time he sold hardware and implements. He spent a couple of years in the dry goods business. He also had a ranch on the side. Eventually he concentrated solely on his ranch and farming interests.

S. W. Crutcher reached the age of 84 years. In June 1928 he passed away and is buried in Sweetwater. One further facet of the Crutcher family presents itself in Charles W. Crutcher. He was a World War I veteran and spent three years or more at the Veteran's

Hospital in Sawrelle, California, a suburb of Los Angeles. He took up short story and scenario writing as an occupation. In 1927 he had a collection of stories published under the title, "Tales of Topango." It is named after a canyon in California called Topango.

His book helped him become connected with Universal Studios as a scenario writer. At the time of his father's death in 1928, Charles was collaborating with B. M. Bower,[56] a novelist with over sixty western books to her credit at the time. Plans were to film all sixty.

Crutcher and his co-workers were writing on "Chip of the Flying U," the next film in the series, when Charles was called home for his father's funeral.[57]

California Death Records show that Charles died in Los Angeles in 1973.[58] The writer has also found Crutchers who are writing at Universal today. One can only wonder if they might be descendants of Samuel Crutcher.

It appears unusual to the writer that Sam and his sons fought in three of the nations wars in one lifetime. Sam fought in the Civil War, Tom in the Spanish-American War, and Charles in World War One.

Shortly after The Difficulty, Thadeus Hanes moved his shop to Shamrock. He became a Justice of the Peace there and remained so until his death in 1894. He is buried in Liberty Cemetery.

Store and saloonkeeper Franklin Dillard is also buried at Liberty Cemetery with his wife.

Enoch Hooten, a Justice of the Peace along with George B. Leachman, remained a Justice of the Peace in Mexico until his death in 1894. One of Enoch's sons, Robert, was a Justice of the Peace for his lifetime also.

John W. Crigler and his wife, Sarah, moved to Mexico, Missouri in 1894. In 1895 John died of pneumonia.

One of John's sons by his first wife, Walter, the 14-year-old who walked with his Uncle Milton the night before Milton was killed, became a schoolteacher and started a successful school in New Harman, Tennessee, about ten miles from Shelbyville, Tennessee. Lebbeus or "Leb", his brother, was a lawyer in Mexico, St. Louis, and later moved to Shelbyville, Tennessee also.

Milton Scott's sister, Sarah Frances Crigler, lived to be nearly 90 years old. She was, perhaps, the longest lived of those associated with The Difficulty. She died on the 25th of February 1930 and is buried beside her husband at Elmwood Cemetery in Mexico.

In 1871 Sam bought a lot in Martinsburgh across the street from his tin shop, which was on the north side of Washington Street. This lot was owned by William H. Morris.[58] It is the present location of N. Fennewald Pump Service. The writer believes that Sam

18

built the building that later became the shop of long time tinner, Andrew Pihale. Norb Fennewald, the founder of the pump service, bought the building from Pihale. The building was later moved to Danville. One can still see the old shop key on the wall at the pump service. Did Sam carry this key in his pocket every morning to open up? The writer believes he did.

(Sam Crutcher's) Andrew Pihale's Tin Shop, Martinsburg, MO

Dr. S. M. Dodson's Drug Store was west of Sam's tin shop at the time of The Difficulty. It was supposed to have been built from lumber from a traveling circus, which failed in Martinsburg. It was constructed on railroad ground. Jacobi & Sons were using it as a furniture storage warehouse in 1926. Joseph Muster, a long time Martinsburg resident, said that enough alcohol had been consumed in it to float a steamboat.[59]

Endnotes
[1]Stewart Sifakis, Compendium of the Confederate Armies; Kentucky, Maryland, Missouri, the Confederate Units and the Indian Units (New York: Facts On File Books, 1995), p. 127.
    The 11th Regiment, formerly Burns' 8th Regiment, was organized during the winter of 1863-1864. The unit served in Parson's and S. P. Burns' Brigade, Trans-Mississippi Department, and fought in Arkansas and Louisiana. It fought at Pleasant Hill and Jenkins Ferry. Early in 1865 it disbanded.
    [2]Monroe County, Missouri Historical Society, Monroe County,

<u>Missouri... Then and Now 1831-2006</u> (Evansville,IN: M. T. Publishing Co., Inc., 2006), p. 189.

Ambrose came to Monroe County with his parents and brother, Samuel. Charles, his father, was known for sowing the first wheat in the county. Ambrose developed a deep green watermelon known as the "Crutcher melon." It was very popular with the local farmers.

Ambrose was also a master blacksmith. Young men came to him to learn the trade. Nimrod Ashcraft was such a man. At eighteen in 1850 he apprenticed himself to Mr. Crutcher and is shown living with him on the census of that year. The first two years he received thirty dollars a year. The third year he was paid fifty dollars. Out of that three-year apprenticeship Nimrod saved twenty dollars, which was enough to start him in business.

[3]_____. History of Audrain County, Missouri (St. Louis: National Historical Co., 1884), p. 266. Hereinafter cited as History of Audrain.

[4]"State of Missouri vs. William R. Martin, Sr., Perjury," 1866, Audrain County, Missouri Circuit Court Tills, Till #140, Case No. 30, Case Files 1837-1883. Audrain County Area Genealogical Society, 305 West Jackson St., Mexico, Audrain County, Missouri. Microfilm No. C37565.

Southerners generally never used the term Civil War. They referred to the conflict as the War Between the States or the War for Southern Independence. After the war the idea of southern independence was scrapped and the name War Between the States became more popular in the south.

Martinsburgh was a hotbed of southern sympathy. William R. Martin, the founder, was said to have helped raised a Confederate flag in Martinsburgh on the fifth of April 1861. This was a full week before the opening guns of the war at Sumpter. This act along with several utterances against the Union made him suspect when he swore an oath that he was loyal for the purpose of voting in 1866. Because of this an indictment was brought against him for perjury. He died before the case was brought to trial.

[5]History of Audrain, p. 266.

[6]"Testimony of Elizabeth Hall, Crutcher-Tapscott Murder Case," 1871, Audrain County Circuit Tills, Till #229, Case No. 1, Case Files 1837-1883, no page nos. Audrain County Area Genealogical Society, 305 West Jackson St., Mexico, Audrain County, MO. Microfilm No. C37573. Hereinafter cited as Circuit Court Till #229.

[7]"Testimony of Elizabeth Hall," Circuit Court Till #229. No page nos.

[8]"Testimony of Elizabeth Hall," Circuit Court Till #229. No

20

page nos.

[9]"Testimony of Elizabeth Hall," Circuit Court Till #229. No page nos.

[10]"Testimony of Augustus Tapscott," Circuit Court Till #229. No page nos.

[11]"Testimony of Augustus Tapscott," Circuit Court Till #229. No page nos.

[12]"Testimony of Augustus Tapscott," Circuit Court Till #229. No page nos.

[13]History of Audrain, p. 266.

[14]"Burials in the Old Martinsburg Cemetery, 1868-1871," Audrain County Cemeteries, Audrain County Area Genealogical Society, 305 West Jackson St., Mexico, Audrain County, MO, Book 5 Mace thru New Mount Z.

A niece of Milton Scott, Alice N. Crigler Davis, wife of James M. Davis, age 20, died 12 April 1871. She was buried on her father's, John Crigler's, land in what is known today as the Old Martinsburg Cemetery. She joined three young ex-Confederates, who were shot down in Martinsburg in 1868. Milton himself was buried there in August 1871. Two months later another of Crigler's daughters and a niece of Milton's, Susan A., age 18, was buried in the little cemetery. Death at a young age was not at all unusual.

[15]"Testimony of Robert Farthing," Circuit Court Till #229. No page nos.

[16]"Testimony of Robert Armstrong," Circuit Court Till #229. No page nos.

[17]"Testimony of David Rice," Circuit Court Till #229. No page nos.

[18] It would be interesting to know why he "went below" and returned. He did say the next day that he had a friend up the road and one in St. Louis to do the dirty work for him. This was a rather cryptic statement.

[19]"Testimony of Samuel Crutcher," Circuit Court Till #229. No page nos.

[20]"Testimony of Charles B. Clark," Circuit Court Till #229. No page nos.

[21]"Testimony of Charles B. Clark," Circuit Court Till #229. No page nos.

[22]"Testimony of Charles B. Clark," Ciucuit Court Till #229. No page nos.

[23]"Testimony of Charles B. Clark," Circuit Court Till #229. No page nos.

[24]"Testimony of Charles B. Clark," Circuit Court Till #229. No page nos.

[25]"Testimony of Daniel Brooks," Circuit Court Till #229. No

page nos.

[26]"Testimony of Thadeus Hanes," Circuit Court Till #229. No page nos.

[27]"Testimony of Thadeus Hanes," Circuit Court Till #229. No page nos.

[28]"Testimony of William H. Martin," Circuit Court Till #229. No page nos.

[29]"Testimony of William H. Martin," Circuit Court Till #229. No page nos.

[30]"Testimony of Thadeus Hanes," Circuit Court Till #229. No page nos.

[31]"Testimony of Thadeus Hanes," Circuit Court Till #229. No page nos. Thad Hanes testified that Milton Scott had said several times that if he did not get him (Crutcher) today he would get him.

[32]"Testimony of Sam Crutcher," Circuit Court Till #229. No page nos.

[33]Quoits is a game involving the throwing of metal rings over a set distance to land over a pin (nob) in the center of a clay patch. Quoits weigh from three to ten pounds. The game is very similar to the pitching of horseshoes.

[34]"Testimony of Frank Dillard," Circuit Court Till #229. No page nos.

[35]"Testimony of Thomas Preston," Circuit Court Till #229. No page nos.

[36]"Testimony of Thomas Preston," Circuit Court Till #229. No page nos.

[37]"Testimony of Sam Crutcher," Circuit Court Till #229. No page nos.

[38]"Testimony of Dr. M. M. Tucker," Circuit Court Till #229. No page nos.

[39]"Testimony of Dr. M. M. Tucker," Circuit Court Till #229. No page nos.

[40]"Testimony of Dr. M. M. Tucker," Circuit Court Till #229. No page nos.

[41]"Testimony of Dr. M. M. Tucker," Circuit Court Till #229. No page nos.

[42]The sum of one thousand dollars for the recognizance of S. W. Crutcher was secured by D. D. Woodward and James M. Harrison. The securities for A. W. Tapscott were James M. Harrison and E. P. French.

Sheriff White charged $1.00 for each arrest and $21.00 for two guards for 7 days at $1.50 per day each. Also charged were seven days of service for the sheriff himself, $14.00; boarding prisoners and guards for seven days, $35.00; Mileage to arrest and return, 28 miles, $2.08; Summons for witness, .50; Calling 47 witnesses

@ .05 each, $2.35; total cost, $73.93.

Thadeus Hanes, Constable of Loutre Township, also turned in a bill of cost. Constable fee serving subpoenas and mileage, $13.95; serving warrant to S. W. Crutcher, .75; serving warrant to A. W. Tapscott, .75; two more subpoenas, .70; total cost, $16.15.

[43]On the 15th of August the defendants reappeared in court and their recognizance was raised to two thousand dollars each. J. L. Cartmell and Nathan Dix provided the securities for the men.

[44]Circuit Attorney C. E. Peers later moved to Warrenton. In March of 1888 he was appointed to fill a vacancy on the bench of the St. Louis Court of Appeals.

[45]"Court Document of Justice Enoch Hooten," Circuit Court Till #229. No page nos.

[46]There is no indication whether the following list of fees applied to the Grand Jury session or a court trial. G. B. Leachman, J. P., fee for Warrant, .70; 7 subpoenas, $2.45; adjourned twice, .70; swaring [sic] 20 witnesses, $1.00; Siting [sic] 8 days $2.00 per day, $16.00; journy [sic] to Mexico, $2.00; total of $22.50.

(Witnesses were paid $4.00 each with two exceptions; M. M. Tucker, nonresident, received $10.00 and $8.00 for 100 miles mileage; Joseph Dunn, two days, $1.00.) The following is a witness list of which only 20 were sworn; W. H. Martin, L. Wilson, B. E. Carver, T. L. Preston, J. S. Muster, A. J. Torreyson, F. S. Frier, J. C. Martan, Woodson Randel, H. P. Eckler, F. Dillard, J. Wooldridge, D. B. Rice, G. A. Burwell, B. G. Beckett, D. T. Owens, H. H. Washburn, Jacob Cartmell, S. M. Dodson, John Taylor, W. B. Right, J. M. Tucker, C. B. Clark, James Woourly, T. W. Hains, James Haislip, and R. Armstrong. (Spelled as written).

[47]"Oral interview with Joe Vance," 19 Aug 2007, by Paul Hoer, St. Joseph Catholic Cemetery, Martinsburg, Missouri. Mr. Vance visited Crutcher Cemetery in 1983 and recorded the stones. His handwritten description and notes are found in the cemetery book at the Monroe County Historical Society, Paris, Monroe County, MO.

There is a problem with the death date of Clara Tapscott Crutcher as shown on her tombstone and the birthdate of Thomas Crutcher taken from the Nolan County, Texas Death Records, Book 5, p. 237. Her death is recorded as 17 Feb 1876. His birthdate is recorded as 20 Aug 1876. This is an obvious impossibility. She probably died in childbirth. Dates are very fluid and it is not unusual to see this type of error.

[48]"Evidence of interest in Texas in the 1870s," Mexico Weekly Ledger, (Mexico, Audrain County, MO), 21 Dec 1876, Thursday, Vol. 18, No. 35, p. 4, col. 1. Hereinafter cited as Mexico Ledger.

"Texas Muddle---'Texas or bust' has been the motto of some

for the past few weeks and last night some of them went to Texas and some did not, so of course they busted. We would love to tell something definite, but they don't know themselves and so we of course have to wait developments. We refrain from expressing our opinion of this enterprise just now, but we are in a condition to know the truth in a few weeks, and will give it as it is, for we will have a reporter on the grant and as soon as we can, we will inform the public whether all this is moonshine or not."

[49]1880 U. S. Census, Precinct 1, Brown County, Texas; p. 377, National Archives Roll: T9_1292; Family History Film: 1255292. William H. Martin, 47, Drug Dealer; Martha A., 42, Ada L., 14, Jas. W., 12. The Martin families that occasionally visit Martinsburg stem from this Martin line.

[50]"Former Citizen Here from Dallas, Texas," Martinsburg Monitor (Martinsburg, Audrain County, MO), 15 Jun 1933, Thursday, Vol. 14, No. 34, p. 1, col. 2. "The only business houses left are the building occupied by Joe G. Fennewald, which was then the bank and the Jacobi Furniture Department, then Dr. Dodson's Drug Store. The only houses still standing are the residence of Miss Margaret Torreyson and the old Muster house."

[51]"Genealogy of Martha Della 'Mattie' Houser Pearce Crutcher," Descendants of Martha Elizabeth Baber/James Houser [database online], 27 Mar 2006. www.baberfamilytree.org/usa/baber-houser. htm (Accessed 10 Oct 2006), p. 2.

[52]History of Audrain, p. 266.

[53]Mexico Ledger, "Stray Notice," 16 Nov 1876, Thursday, Vol. 18, No. 30, p. 6, col. 5. "Taken up by Thomas S. Pearson, on the 1st November 1876, one bay mare, with white spot in the forehead; about two years old past. No other marks or brands perceivable; and appraised at $40, by Hiram Blivin and S. C. Hale, and posted before the undersigned justice on the 4th of Nov., 1876. A. W. Tapscott, J. P."

[54]Mexico Ledger, "Marriage Notice," 15 Mar 1883, Thursday, Vol. 24, No. 48, p. 3, col. 4. "On the 7th inst., 4 miles north of Martinsburg, by Squire Tapscott, John Howard and Miss Ellen Nichols. All of Audrain."

"Marriage of John Howard and Ellen Nichols," 7 Mar 1883, Audrain County Marriages, Audrain County Genealogical Society, 305 West Jackson St., Mexico, Audrain County, Missouri, Book 1, p. 156.

[55]"Obituary for Thomas E. Crutcher," The Nolan County News (Sweetwater, Nolan County, Texas), 20 Jul 1937, p. 1. Hereinafter cited as Nolan County News.

[56]Between 1906 and 1940, Bertha M. Bower, wrote 68 novels set in the American West. Born Bertha Muzzy in Minnesota

in 1871, Bower moved with her family to Montana. She taught school in the Great Falls area. At 19 she married her first husband, C. J. Bower. She began writing short stories in 1900 but did not have much success until her novel, "Chip of the Flying U" was published in 1906. She published novels regularly until her death in 1940. Many of her novels were adapted to film.

"Biographical sketch of Bower," B. M. Bower Collection, Western History Collections, University of Oklahoma, Norman, OK, p. 1. www.lib.ou.edu/etc/westhist/bower/index.asp

[57]Nolan County News, "Obituary of S. W. Crutcher," 21 Jun 1928, p. 1.

[58]"Warranty Deed of William H. Morris to Samuel Crutcher," 29 April 1871 (filed 4 Sep 1871), Audrain County Deed Records, Book 3, p. 553. Audrain County Recorder's Office, Audrain County Courthouse, Mexico, Audrain Co., MO.

[59]Rev. Henry Freese, comp., Historical Scetches of the Town of Martinsburg, Missouri and It's Institutions, A Souvenir of Martinsburg, MO 1926, Issued on the occasion of the Golden Jubilee of St. Joseph's Church, October, 1926. Original copy in possession of writer.

Crumbs

Martinsburg Monitor (Martinsburg, Audrain County, MO), Thursday. 7 Jul 1932, Vol. 13, No. 37, p. 1, col. 2.

HISTORIC FOURTH OF JULY CELEBRATION IN MARTINSBURG IN 1898

In 1898 a Fourth of July celebration and picnic was held at Crigler's Grove, one-half mile south of Martinsburg, which has gone down in history as the biggest community celebration ever held here.

At ten o'clock in the morning the parade started from the town hall to the picnic ground, headed by the Martinsburg Brass Band. Next in line followed an immense float, entirely covered with flags and bunting, on which rode young ladies, dressed in white and each one representing a state of the Union, displayed on a conspicuous sash. Next came the imposing carriage with Uncle Sam in the person of N. M. Callaway, who was well fitted for the part. Miss Maragarette Torreyson, who rode in the next carriage represented Miss Columbia.

Hundreds of carriages of all kinds joined in the parade, many beautifully decorated in the national colors.

Arrived at the picnic grounds the Declaration of Independence was read by "Miss Columbia." Then a group of patriotic songs was sung, by the assembled chorus, under the direction of F. G. Jacobi. Then began the Speaking program.

Among the prominent speakers and visitors from a distance were: David E. Francis,[1] St. Louis; R. D. Cowherd, Kansas City; Sam Cook, Mexico, and a number of candidates seeking important state offices.

In the afternoon came the news of the grand victory of Admiral Dewey, over the Spanish fleet in Manila Bay. When the telegram was read the vast throng broke into long and loud cheering and the band struck up the Star Spangled Banner.

That night $300.00 worth of fireworks were shot off on the depot grounds and a number of balloons were sent up.

The picnic was a grand success and had been unequaled in the 34 years that have passed since.   (by F.G. Jacobi)

[1]former Governor of Missouri

Mexico Weekly Ledger (Mexico, Audrain County, MO),
26 Jun 1890, Thursday, Vol. 32, No. 12, p. 4, col. 4.

Horses Killed
From the Martinsburg Message

During the storm Wednesday a very valuable team of horses belonging to Jeff Cunningham was struck by lightning and killed instantly. This was Mr. Cunningham's best team, and is quite a heavy loss. The horses were valued at about $200.

A fine team belonging to Mr. Albert W. Martin, valued at about $250, was killed by lightning during the storm here Wednesday.

Mexico Weekly Ledger (Mexico, Audrain County, MO),
26 Mar 1896, Thursday, Vol. 38, No. 52, p. 3, col. 7.

MARTINSBURG ITEMS

We have a new band, the Union Cornet, in our midst, composed of young men in the Catholic church. Their names are as follows: John Adrian, Ben Bertels, Henry Fennewald, Adolph Fennewald, Jr., Ben Fennewald, Steve Beuscher, Jr., Henry Beuscher, Jr., Ben Beuscher, Frank Mispagel, and Ben Kimno [sic]. These young men serenaded Fathers Haar and Deil one night last week, after which they were entertained very pleasantly in the priest's home.

Mexico Weekly Ledger (Mexico, Audrain County, MO),
9 Apr 1896, Thursday, Vol. 38, No. 2, p. 3, col. 7.

MARTINSBURG ITEMS

Several young folks from Benton attended the Easter entertainment at the Christian Church Saturday night. Among them were Misses Dodie and Fannie Tratchel, Prof. H. Painter, and Albert Davis.[1]

[1]Fannie Tratchel and Albert Davis later married. They were the parents of Albert Lee Davis.

Mexico Intelligencer (Mexico, Audrain County, MO), 28 Jan 1886, Thursday, Vol. 14, No. 43, p. 1, col. 4.

REAL ESTATE TRANSFERS

George Robertson to Geo. H. Edwards,[1]
Lot 40X120 feet. Lot 1, block 5, Laddonia, $495. Quit claim deed.
J. S. Rollins to Wm. Ayers,[2]
Lots 1, 2, and 4, block 5, Benton City, $85.
[1]See George H. Edwards in Slice 9.
[2]J. S. Rollins was a prominent historical person in Boone County.

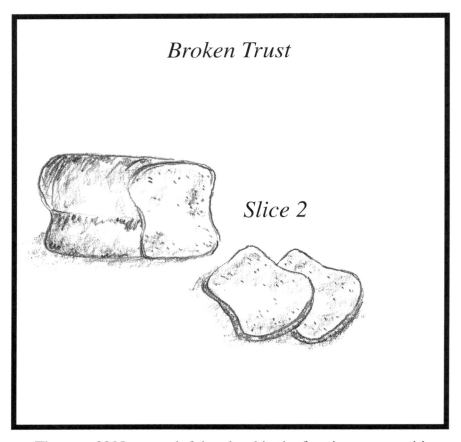

Broken Trust

Slice 2

The year 2009 was painful and sad in the farming communities of eastern Audrain County, Missouri. When the state closed down T. J. Gieseker Trucking, along with its grain buying operation because of irregularities, farmers were heavily impacted. As of this writing, Cathy Gieseker, owner and operator, has pled guilty to Federal charges. On February 25th, 2010 she was sentenced to nine years in prison. State charges are still pending.[1]

The economic losses of $27.4 million were staggering. As this financial loss rippled through the community the results were many and varied. Although the full story has not yet emerged, people hope these facts will come out in a forthcoming trial.

Historically, this is not the first time such an event took place in Audrain County, Missouri. Less than two miles in distance and eighty-four years in time, in 1926, the crash of the Fennewald Brothers plunged this same area into economic chaos. It might be relevant to review the happenings of that era and realize the destruction of trust that took place, and the suffering that those involved endured.

The breakdown of trust is a long-lived phenomena. Even though all of the principals of the 1926 event are deceased, there are still vestiges of the reaction that took place in evidence today. Some enmity's still exist among families that they might not even realize stem back to that time. Warnings passed down by parents to their children through generations were formulated as a result of that broken trust.

In the fall 1926, George H. Fennewald commented upon the situation he had created. "It's a crying shame! Look at them all around – friends who lent me their money because I was 'good for it' and now I'm broke and can't pay them back."[2]

At the time George spoke, fourteen suits had been filed against George, his twin brother, Frank, and Frank's wife, Elizabeth. His neighbors, family, even a St. Louis priest, banks, and commission houses all wanted to attach property and/or collect on their notes.

George's father, Barney Fennewald, moved to the settlement at Martinsburg in 1873 and became a prairie pioneer. He had been working for an Illinois farmer, who urged him to take up some prairie land he had for sale. When he came to Martinsburg he had just married in Osage County and left the next day to come to the land he had purchased, located in Audrain County. He settled to the hard work of building a farm and rearing a family. Along the way he earned a reputation that the word of a Fennewald was as good as his bond.

By 1882 he had a fine brick home and was known for his acuity in feeding livestock.[3] He brought his family up in the ways of hard work and financial thrift.

In January 1926, an article in the Martinsburg Monitor offered high praise to Barney Fennewald for his success as a feeder for 55 years. Over 80 years old he had just sold a consignment of steers on the St. Louis Market and was preparing to buy another string for the summer markets.[4]

A Globe-Democrat article gave an explanation of the extraordinary credit opportunities offered to any person named Fennewald.[5]

George and Frank, twin sons of Barney Fennewald, following the lessons of their father, acquired large farms and raised corn, oats, and hay. These crops went into their business of fattening cattle and hogs for the St. Louis markets.

George had a 320-acre farm, some of the best land in the community.[6] Frank had a farm and rented another one for his operation.

In the business of feeding it was necessary to buy grain futures to cover anticipated needs as a way of protecting oneself against rising grain prices. In a small way this is speculation.

The article in the Globe-Democrat stated, "the old generation always let it end there – it gave them protection on the fat cattle and hogs they sold on the future delivery plan themselves and frequently saved them quite a big expense in rising corn markets."[7]

George strayed from the tried and true methods of the area's feeders. As a young man he began dabbling in the Board of Trade speculations. By his own admission it was a fascination with the game that grew within him. He had a vision of wealth, easily obtained, that was an age-old draw to speculate.

Although it was not generally well known, George was broken by the market once before. The money lost at that time, during the war (World War I), was George's own. The community was not aware of his misfortune.

After World War One, the markets improved and George's fortunes rebounded. He built a sum estimated to have been $85,000.

He was married in 1921 at St. Nicholas Church in St. Louis.[8] He wed Teresa Adrian, daughter of Henry and Catherine Morfeld Adrian. He vowed to himself to stop playing the market. His steadfastness to stop was shaken by his tax bill. He owed the government $11,500 for one year.

Upon reflection he decided to enter the market one last time, to recoup what he had to pay the government in taxes.

He began feeding money into the market. No profits were forthcoming. He involved his twin brother, Frank. The losses mounted.

George averred, "I bought wheat at $1.73 ½ and the brokers kept telling me all the time that it would see $2 or $2.25.[9]

Frank helped get loans from his friends and signed notes at the bank. The unlimited credit that the Fennewald name had built up was in full play. The community gave them all the extra money they had.

George complained, "My friends, my neighbors, from whom I had borrowed money for short terms for stock feeding operations, would object to taking their money back again. 'Keep it George, if you can use it,' they would say...[10] George was allowing them six percent interest while the banks were only paying four.

It did not seem to occur to the lenders, that if the Fennewalds were amassing a fortune in the market, why would they need to borrow large sums of money? The people seemed blinded by the higher interest rates.

Even the banks were giving easy credit because of the Fennewald name. When interest became overdue and notes went unpaid, even more credit was extended. Frank was allowed by a bank to sign his wife's name to notes without her knowledge.

Mexico's First National Bank, the Mexico Savings Bank, the

Farmer's Bank of Laddonia, the Bank of Laddonia, the Martinsburg Bank, the Rush Hill Bank, and the Wellsville Bank all approved loans to the brothers. Nearly every friend or neighbor of the Fennewalds had money on loan to them.

A deposition given by George H. Fennewald in the fall of 1926 revealed that a meeting with the First National Bank of Mexico and the Martinsburg Bank had taken place prior to the first suit being filed.

The First National Bank held a $9,700 note and the Martinsburg Bank had an $8,700 note. These notes were overdue. They discussed with George what could legally be done as far as collection of these notes. George's father, Barney, was included in these deliberations. He agreed to assume the two notes. He took an $11,000 mortgage on the 320-acre homestead. Barney surrendered two promissary notes totaling $8,925 held against George and he accepted a deed for the farm. As the Ledger stated, "This was one of Audrain County's showplace farms.[11]

Even before any of the suits had been filed, the legality of this transfer had been questioned. Those that filed suits were confounded by this fact.

George's defense was, "I wanted, above all else, to protect my father in what I owed him, ahead of any other creditors.[12]

In the spring of 1926, the crash began with a $300 lawsuit filed by Mrs. Mary Seckler, a widow. When this action was undertaken and the public became aware, there was a rush to file. Joseph F. Fennewald, Liborius Ahrens, John Madden, Joseph H. Fennewald, Helen Schneider, Mary A. Fennewald, Bartlett-Frazier Co., Joe Burston, Jacob Freyer, Bank of Laddonia, Bank of Rush Hill, Bank of Martinsburg brought suits against Frank and one against Elizabeth. Fourteen suits in all were filed.

Because he had transferred the farm, George had nothing left to pay his indebtedness. Barney rented the farm to George's wife, Teresa. George farmed the land. He was sad he could not pay his friends. His only choice was to work for years and earn a profit he could turn over for repayment.

The effect of the crash was much harsher on George's brother, Frank. Frank's involvement was to shore up his brother's failing fortunes. He played the grain futures to some extent and with the same result as his brother had, losses. His attempts, however, to aid his brother took him in even deeper. He, too, borrowed from all his friends and family. The banks allowed him to sign his wife's name to notes. When her name appeared in the suits she had no idea why. She had not known that her husband had speculated. She had been against speculation in the past.

As the suits were filed in circuit court the disgrace weighed heavily on Frank. As the sums he had borrowed added up he couldn't believe the amounts. Frank's health crumbled, he had a nervous breakdown and was hospitalized in Fulton.

By July 1st, 1926 Frank's 160-acre farm (NE ¼ , Sect. 30, Twp. 51, Range 6W) was to be auctioned at the courthouse door.[13] Elizabeth and her eight children had to hang on somehow. The newspaper pointed out that she was the daughter of the late Mr. & Mrs. Henry Paschang. When Henry died in 1910 her mother managed the family's affairs as her mother did before her. Mrs. Antonette Kuensting's husband died in 1869, and she was responsible for her family for 34 years. Elizabeth, it was told, came from a family famous for its women managers.[14] Her oldest sons, twins, 21-years-old, were prepared to keep the family together.

Many in the family came to the aid of their brothers. Barney's help was substantial and controversial. His actions preserved George's farm but removed any chance for compensation for those who had lost money. The writer tracked the trials of suits and found none that ended with the plaintiffs winning. An example of such a case was reported in the newspaper in October, 1926. It was titled, "Fennewald Gets Verdict in Case, A verdict for the defendant was returned by the jury which heard the case of Helen Schneider vs. George Fennewald in circuit court here Friday and Saturday. The suit was one on attachment."[15]

While many in the community were angered by their losses, some were sympathetic and railed against the Chicago Board of Trade. They attacked the business practices of the Board and the unscrupulous brokers who lured people into a financial trap.

Others whose money was gone felt it was foolish to try to recoup it. They did not take legal action because they felt there was no chance of recovering anything.

"Another group in whom the personal word of either (brother) was sufficient security for a loan, have neither signature nor written document to show for their reputed loans.[16]

In summary, then, there were those who helped Frank and George. They remained favorable to them. Next were the ones who were angry and brought suit in circuit court. Another group felt it was useless to try to squeeze blood out of a turnip. Finally, there were the ones who could not prove their claims because they had no documentation.

Out of this grew a wide range of emotions and actions that had a long lasting effect. Some lessons were obviously not learned to produce these types of financial collapses. Greed was the trigger that allowed the disaster to grow. It was not realized that greed has a cost. To repay these costs may take generations.

The effects of these conditions were long lived and and diverse.

One cannot begin to calculate what it will be, who will touched by it, and how far that effect will reach into the future. There is also a human cost in mental anguish, worry, anger, and negative financial conditions or hard times.

In the Fennewald case the newspaper summed it up well. "For the grain markets got this money (George and Frank's investment), which George and Frank borrowed from friends and acquaintances on the strength of unlimited credit the family had. Got not only the money, but Frank's health, too; and George's bright outlook and plans for his boy and girl; got Mrs. Elizabeth Fennewald's happiness in her home and hopes for the family of eight children; now thrown on their own resources, destroyed the joy that old Barney Fennewald now above his eightieth year, had always taken in his two successful sons; destroyed the respect and honor of the Fennewald name, took everything, hook, line, and sinker."[17]

Frank's health never recovered. On the second of June 1930 he fell into a concrete cattle-watering tank and drowned. He weighed 90 pounds and was so weak that it was generally believed that he could not get out of the tank. He was 55.

Death claimed George's wife, Teresa, in 1930. She was 43. She was buried in Westphalia, MO, the town where she was born instead of the Fennewald plots at Martinsburg. Frank and Teresa were part of the cost that had to be paid. Her burial in Westphalia makes one wonder if that too, was an effect of the situation.

The only piece of property sold off the courthouse steps belonged to Frank.[18] It was purchased by Samuel Fendrick. It remains in the Fendrick family today.

Endnotes

[1]Mexico Ledger (Mexico, Audrain County, MO), 26 Feb 2010, Friday, Vol. 156, No. 40, p. 1, cols. 5,6.
[2]Mexico Intelligencer (Mexico, Audrain County, MO), 15 Jul 1926, Thursday, Vol. 68, No. 134, p. 4, cols. 3,4,5,6. Reprint of a Globe-Democrat article. Hereinafter cited as Intelligencer.
[3]_____. History of Audrain County, Missouri (St. Louis: National Historical Co., 1884), pp. 564,565.
[4]Martinsburg Monitor (Martinsburg, Audrain County, MO), 21 Jan 1926, Thursday, Vol. 7, No. 9, p. 1, col. 2. Hereinafter cited as the Monitor.
[5]Intelligencer, 15 Jul 1926,Vol. 68, No. 134, p. 4.
[6]Intelligencer, p. 4.
[7]Intelligencer, p. 4.
[8]Intelligencer, 13 Jan 1921, Vol. 68, No. 49, p. 1.
[9]Intelligencer, 15 Jul 1926, Vol. 68, No. 134, p. 4.
[10]Mexico Weekly Ledger (Mexico, Audrain County, MO), 24

Jun 1926, Thursday, Vol. 68, No. 19, p. 5, cols. 2,3. Hereinafter cited as Mexico Weekly Ledger.
[11]Mexico Weekly Ledger, p. 5.
[12]Mexico Weekly Ledger, p. 5.
[13]Laddonia Herald (Laddonia, Audrain County, MO), 9 Jun 1926, Vol. 42, No. 11, p. 2, col. 2. Hereinafter cited as the Herald.
[14]Mexico Weekly Ledger, 24 Jun 1926, Vol. 68, No. 19, p. 5.
[15]Intelligencer, 14 Oct 1926, Vol. 68, No. 147, p. 3.
[16]Herald, p. 2.
[17]Intelligencer, 15 Jul 1926, Vol. 68, No. 134, p. 4.
[18]Herald, p. 2.

Crumbs

Mexico Weekly Ledger (Mexico, Audrain County, MO),
11 Jul 1889, Thursday, Vol. 31, No. 14, p. 1, col. 9.

A Martinsburg Mystery
Lightning's Strange Work in a Church –
An Electrician's Queer Story

In the Columbia Herald of this week, Mr. J. L. Carnes, an electrical expert, tells the following strange story of the lightning's work in a church at Martinsburg, east of here.

"Martinsburg, a little town, situated on the Wabash railroad, in the eastern edge of Audrain county, some three or four years ago was visited by a terrific thunderstorm, and a new church building[1] was struck by lightning, the effect of which is, without exception, the strangest freak of lightning that ever came under my observation. There is one flue in the center of the roof, a stove on either side of the building – pipes running together at the ceiling both entering the same flue. The lightning struck the flue, scattering brick in every direction. The whole force of the stroke ran down one stove pipe, and when it reached the stove, which stood some five feet from the wall, the entire force of the electricity flashed against the plastering, blackening it over a surface of perhaps five or six feet square. In the center of this blackened place was a well defined photograph of a man – the features plain and distinct. It represented a man apparently about sixty years old with long hair
34

and whiskers, both streaming back over the shoulders, as if the man was being hurled through the air at the rate of sixty miles an hour. An artist of the town[2] took his apparatus and photographed the scene, and has sold thousands of the photographs. Hundreds have seen this picture on the wall and will verify this statement.[3]

[1]St. Joseph Catholic Church was built in 1886 and was the new church building struck by lightning.

[2]The artist/photographer of the town was N. M. Friedman, owner of Friedman's Picture Frame Factory.

[3]It would be interesting for the people of Audrain County to search their old pictures to see if they discover this old photograph.

Martinsburg Monitor (Martinsburg, Audrain County, MO), 27 Nov 1924, Thursday, Vol. 6, No. 1, p. 1, col. 2.

BRIDGE IS COMPLETED

The bridge 3 ½ miles northwest of Martinsburg in Fennewald School District was completed last week by Henry Dubbert with his able assistants, George Kemna, Road Overseer, Frank Kemna, Clarence Fennewald, Everett Welch, Sylvester Borgmeyer and A. H. Bertels.

Mexico Intelligencer (Mexico, Audrain County, MO), 28 Jan 1886, Thursday, Vol. 14, No. 43, p. 1, col. 4.

REAL ESTATE TRANSFERS

P. H. Gantt to S. V. Overbagh, lot 10x60 feet, part lot 2, block 13, original town of Martinsburg, $25.

Local Story of a Tree

A tree on the prairie is an important landmark. This is illustrated in a local story told about Walter Tratchel, Benton City.

Walter was a soldier in the Union signal corps[1] from Ohio during the Civil War. After the war he obtained a farm in Audrain County eastnortheast of Benton City. It was located in Section 6, Township 50N, Range 7W.[2] It lay about a mile north of the North Missouri Railroad's right-of-way.

The farm was said to have a tree. When Walter walked east out of Mexico down the track towards Martinsburg, he was able to find his land because he could see the tree.

In the early days, paths through the tall prairie grass in the vicinity of Tratchel's led to the farmstead, because people could see the tree. Anyone passing by always visited Walter and Sarah.

Is the story absolutely true? The writer does not know. It does, however, show the obvious importance of a tree on the prairie.

[1]National Park Service. U.S. Civil War Soldiers 1861-1865 [database on-line], Provo, UT, USA: Ancestry.com Operations Inc, 2007. Accessed 15 Apr 2011.

[2]_____. An Illustrated Historical Atlas of Audrain County, Missouri (Philadelphia: Edwards Bros., 1877) p. 18.

Mexico Weekly Ledger (Mexico, Audrain County, MO),
15 Jun 1916, Thursday, Vol. 58, No. 16, p. 4, col. 6.

Circuit Court News

Charles Muster, who was sentenced to six months in jail for violating the local option laws (drinking) was paroled Saturday on condition that he leave the state immediately.

James Corder was paroled.

John Gillespie was fined $25 for gambling.[1]

[1]Three Martinsburg men

Missouri Message (Mexico, Audrain County, MO),
19 Jan 1911, Thursday, Vol. 12, No. 9, p. 1, col. 2.

John W. Wright, 81 years of age, a veteran of the Mexican and Civil Wars, died at his home in Wellsville last week. The body was interred at Martinsburg.

Martinsburg Oracle: The directors of the Martinsburg Bank at their regular meeting Friday showed their appreciation to Miss Mary Stevens for calling up the citizens of Martinsburg during the bank robbery of Dec. 17 by presenting her with a ten dollar gold piece.

Thrums

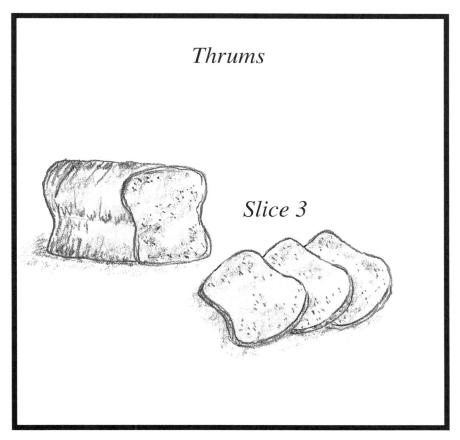

Slice 3

Thrums are small pieces of string, threads, or leftovers! Could a murder trace back to thrums? How could a lingering death connect with pieces of string?

It was a cold day in June of 1859. Two and one half miles straight west[1] of Martinsburg lay the farm of George Washington Crane, Jr. Mary W. was his wife. They were parents of two children; a girl, Augusta Texas and a boy, Walter. There were also two slaves in the household, a rented boy and a girl.

On this cool, damp day George toiled breaking prairie. He wanted to plow forty acres of ground this season. He had been working with mules and whip for days on end. It was the tough work of a pioneer.

Creating new farming ground from the virgin prairie required strong arms, a good whip and dogged persistence. Breaking sod was a laborious job. It took a sharp plow, because the dirt had to be turned upside down to kill the grass. The mules strained to pull the plow through the soil slicing the prairie grass roots. The farmer had to control the plow, guiding it with its handles, keeping it straight. That spring George had paid fifteen cents for the sharping [sic] of the plowe [sic].[2]

The insects were nearly unbearable. The green-headed flies attacked man and beast. Putting up with the bugs was an agony. And one had to keep an eye out for the prairie rattler. This poisonous snake inhabited the grass in considerable numbers. It was a danger to man and mule. The cracking whip was needed to urge the mules forward.

To the north across the rutted path from town lay the farm of Mr. Yates.[3] He, too, was interested in breaking prairie. A hired hand, Alfred M. Carnes, was working at the task for Mr. Yates. While breaking sod at Mr. Yates' farm, Carnes needed a place to board.

Alfred approached Mr. Crane seeking room and board. George agreed to the arrangement. It meant a little added income. Mary Crane later stated, "that she did not care about being troubled with boarders, but after her husband had taken him in she said nothing about it."[4]

Alfred's room was upstairs in a small house. The Cranes slept downstairs. There was only one room downstairs that was finished. The kitchen was separated from the rest of the house. To get upstairs one would have to go through the bedroom on the first floor and into a hall.

On Friday, the seventeenth of June 1859, just ten days after Alfred began his stay with the Cranes, he took a series of actions that led to a Difficulty.

Mary explained, "Carnes was in the habit of using thrums about his whip."[5] She had given Carnes thrums when he came downstairs that morning to use to repair his whip. Did he mistake this kindness for something more?

During Friday morning, Alfred Carnes came back to the house. He went into the kitchen, a place he had not gone before. The black girl went to Mrs. Crane telling her that Carnes was in the kitchen. Mary went upstairs. She put the black girl to work cleaning the house.

While Mary was upstairs she saw Carnes come out of the kitchen. From that point he could look out over the farm. She then heard him come into her bedroom below. He came into the hall and was at the base of the stairs. Mary was on her way down when he called up. "Madam, is my knife up there?"

Mary answered in the negative. She stepped to the side as he came on. She stated, "I stepped to the side to let him pass. In the place of passing he caught me around the waist. I gave him a push and said, put out [sic], you scamp."[6]

38

Mary went down the stairs, while Carnes went up and then followed her down. He questioned her, asking what she meant by calling him a scamp. When she told him he looked like one, he thought for a minute. He then went out. Mary thought he had gone but when she opened the door he was still standing in the yard. A little later Carnes opened the hall door and stood there some time. Finally he left for work. He went to plow across the road to the north on Mr. Yates' farm.

Mrs. Crane then had visitors. Mrs. Graham, her sister-in-law, had arrived.[7] With company in the house Mary did not tell her husband anything at dinnertime. George went back to the field and stayed unusually late.

Alfred Carnes was the first one to come in to supper. He immediately wanted to know if everyone had gone. He also inquired where Mrs. Crane was. Carnes was incorrect about the identity of this visitor. Mary told Carnes she was in the house. She did not inform him that it was Mrs. Graham not Mrs. Crane who was there. Mary supposed he would not know the difference.

At the supper table Mary told Carnes he would have to wait on himself, as she had not finished her work. He asked if she was mad or anything. She did not reply.

Mary went outside and called Mrs. Graham out. She explained what had happened and asked what she should do.

Following Mrs. Graham's advice Mary told Carnes to get his coat and leave, as she had no further use for him. Alfred asked, "Madam, what does that mean?" She replied, "Sir, I want no words from you." He followed her to the kitchen repeating his question and she repeated her reply.[8]

Carnes went to the hall and made the black boy get his things. He started off to the east. He went a few hundred yards to the house of Morgan Collins about eight o'clock Friday evening.

Morgan Collins later testified, "that he (Carnes) wanted to get board for about two weeks...he had been boarding at Cranes but that some exceptions had been taken."[9]

Morgan invited Carnes to stay and thought that Alfred was very restless. He seemed to be focused toward Crane's house. Collins, however, said that Carnes behaved himself while at his house.

Mrs. Crane deposed, "In the evening when the conversation (with Carnes) took place there was no white person present but Mrs. Graham, myself and little children. I did not inform my husband of the conduct of Carnes when he first came home, but when we went to bed I told my husband..."[10]

Collins informed Carnes on Saturday morning, the eighteenth of June, that there would be A Difficulty between him and Washington Crane. He told Carnes that Washington had been there at

4:30 a.m. after him. One must wonder if Morgan Collins lied to G. W. Crane about where Carnes was at the time of his visit. If the Difficulty had taken place at that time of the morning, there may not have been a loaded pistol involved. Events may have taken an entirely different path. Crane had said to Collins that Carnes had insulted his wife and Morgan passed that information to Carnes. In fear, it was probably here that Carnes loaded his pistol to take with him to town.

Pinkney French, partner in the store of Coil, French and Company, stood behind the counter in the store in Martinsburg.[11] He was chatting with William R. Martin, Martinsburg's founder.

Suddenly the south door of the store burst open and in a rush four men noisily entered. A. M. Carnes was the first. He was retreating, crying out, "Oh God, oh God, oh God," his arms over his head trying to protect himself from the blows being rained down on him by George Crane. Mr. Estill came next, followed by Thomas Crane.

The counter ran north and south in the store. As Carnes backed north the beating by Crane continued. William Martin at first thought Crane was beating the man with a martingale,[12] but soon realized it was something heavier.

As Carnes reached two boxes against the counter he sank down under the blows as Crane got in his last licks.

Martin saw Carnes reach to his side and he saw the flash of a pistol. Crane exclaimed he was shot and sank to the floor. Carnes twisted away and ran out the north door with his pistol in his hand.

Uncle Billy Martin went to the door and shook his stick at Carnes, who was standing 25 or 30 feet away in the street. He yelled at Carnes to go to the depot.[13] He called to his sons to arrest Carnes. Carnes gave up. As he went away he had his hand on his head and looked like he would fall.

Dr. Thomas E. Peery was called to see Washington Crane between ten and twelve. He went to the store where Crane was lying on a mattress. His pulse was feeble and he was in pain. Dr. Peery examined his wound on the left side about three inches below the left breast. He probed three inches into the wound and found that it ranged downwards and inwards. It went into the abdominal cavity. Crane was awake and suffering. Dr. Peery stayed with Crane until six o'clock that evening.

Dr. Burlington D. Brown arrived about one o'clock on the 18th. Crane was suffering extremely. Dr. Brown felt sure the wound would produce Crane's death. Dr. Peery concurred. Dr. Brown stayed with Crane through the night until he died on the nineteenth. Dr. Perry rejoined Dr. Brown that morning.

Crane frequently spoke of himself as a dying man. He repeated

40

that he was going to die in the defense of his wife's character. He believed he was dying in a just cause. Before he died Crane asked Dr. Brown "if he knew the cause that led to this Difficulty."[14] Dr. Brown intimated that he did. It was the last conversation of George Washington Crane, Jr. as he breathed his last.

George Crane's account with Coil, French and Company lists items purchased on the day of the shooting, June 18th. It shows one pair pants, one hickory shirt, four candles, one box of mustard, and one Chamber.[15] He was put on a mattress on the floor and since he was in the store all night the candles were for light. The writer believes the mustard had some medical application. The Chamber was certainly a chamber pot for sanitary use. An additional item shown on the 19th was one bill of shrouding for wrapping the body. Brown and Noel provided the coffin and box for sixteen dollars, also on the 19th.[16]

George Washington Crane, Sr.

George Washington Crane, Sr. lived in Montgomery County, Missouri. He was an early pioneer of Montgomery County coming in 1824 from Kentucky. He was a substantial citizen of the County and had held offices in the local government. He was sheriff and assessor at different times.[17] The family cemetery was also located in Montgomery County. The Crane Cemetery[18] lies west of Mineola on a hill above the Loutre Valley. It was here that the body of George W. Crane, Jr. was brought for burial.

Gravestone of George W. Crane, Jr.,
Crane Cemetery, Mineola, MO

It would have been a long trip by wagon from Martinsburg to the Crane Cemetery. By transporting the corpse on the North Missouri Railroad, the route could have been shortened. It could have been taken to Montgomery City and thence overland to the cemetery.

The Response of the Law

The funeral appears to have taken place on Monday, June 20th. This seems evident in the response of the law. Augustus W. Tapscott, Justice of the Peace for Loutre Township, Audrain County, held court on the Tuesday following the shooting. Capt. Tapscott gathered the witnesses to the Difficulty. James A. Coil, Constable of Loutre Township, brought the prisoner, Alfred M. Carnes.[19]

Augustus began taking depositions and conducting cross-examinations. William R. Martin was the first witness to be introduced and sworn. He related the quick, noisy entry of the subjects and what he had seen in the store. He explained how the powerful licks struck by Crane drove Carnes backward. He informed the court that he did not see the pistol Carnes used until after the flash when the pistol fired. Crane, he believed, was three to six feet away from Carnes, maybe closer. His first thought at the moment was that Crane would be powder-burnt because of the closeness. Martin indicated that when he arrived on Sunday Crane was dead.[20]

In cross-examination Martin was questioned about the weapon Crane used. Martin stated that although he originally thought it to be a martingale, when Crane was lying on the floor he saw that it was a common drover's whip, coiled.

When asked if Thomas Crane was aiding his brother, George, in the attack, the question was objected to and the objection was sustained.

The next question was did Thomas Crane have a pistol when in the store? It was "over rooled[sic]."[21]

William R. Martin signed the deposition. Tapscott dated it 21 June 1859.

Pinkney French was the next witness to depose. He told the same basic story as Martin had. He included that he was the first to go to George Crane and examine the wound he had received. When asked about Thomas Crane having a weapon, his reply was "Thomas Crane had a pistol in his hand."[22]

Doctors Thomas E. Peery and B. D. Brown explained their examinations of the deceased George Crane. Their diagnoses were identical and they agreed the wound would prove fatal. Crane conversed with both men and expressed his knowledge that he knew he was going to die and would die in the defense of his wife.

He informed Dr. Brown the reason he used no other weapon was that he thought he could beat Carnes down but he realized he could not do it.[23]

The next deponent in Tapscott's court was Mary W. Crane. She explained in detail the events that occurred on Friday. When Carnes took her around the waist in the hall she thought it was intentional and couldn't possibly have been accidental. She truly

42

believed that his manner and conduct at the time showed that his intentions were evil.

The reader should be reminded that because the court records were handwritten only answers are shown. The questions, therefore, must be inferred.

Mary explained that the only fire was in the kitchen and there was no rain that morning, only a mist or dew. She was asked to describe where Carnes was breaking prairie. She had to reiterate that it was cold and that Carnes had on a pair of her husband's pants. He had explained, she said, that his pants were cotton and her husband's were wool.

Mary indicated that she had given him thrums for his whip. She couldn't remember if he had his oil coat when he left. The width of the stairway was a topic discussed. She couldn't tell in feet and inches how wide the stairway was.

The court thoroughly investigated where Mr. Crane was plowing. There were two hollows in the field. If he were there he could not see around the house.

She was queried about her visitors on Friday. She explained that it was Thomas Crane, George's brother, and his wife, Martha. The other couple was Martha E. Graham, George's sister, and his sister's husband Alex W. Graham.[24] She was asked how she would bed the family if they stayed all night. She told the court it would be three in a bed with the women in one room and the gentlemen in another. Martha Graham and her two daughters were the only ones who stayed during the day and appear to have left before bedtime.

In analyzing her answers it seems that Carnes was trying to build a case that it was a cold, rainy day. After going to work he got cold and came back to the Crane's to warm up in the kitchen. He needed his knife to fix his whip. He accidentally caught Mary around the waist when he slipped on the stairs. She had asked him to leave because she needed the room to bed her company. He had put on her husband's pants because he was cold.

Colburn Brown was called as a witness because he had just moved in the spring of 1859 from a farm one-quarter of a mile from Crane's.

Brown was able to report on the location of the Crane farm. He mentioned the two sloughs in the field where George was plowing. The larger slough was northwest and the smaller one was southeast. If Crane was in a slough or in a position where the stables or back lot blocked the view he could not see around the house. The court was interested to know that if a person were coming from Mr. Yates' farm he could approach the house unseen.

Colburn was asked about the width of the stairway and he reported it the normal width. In cross-examination he believed it to be three feet wide, enough for two people to pass.

He stated that he saw George after he was shot and before he died. He spoke to him and was sure Crane was aware of his condition.

Mostly the cross-examination was a reiteration of his testimony.

Morgan Collins, Crane's neighbor to the east, was the next witness. He, too, had to explain whether a person at the house could be seen from the field. Also the width of the stairway was commented upon.

He offered the information that George Crane had lost an eye and his vision was impaired. He said Crane often wore specks.

Collins said Carnes told him "if he had done anything to cause exceptions at Mr. Crane's he did not know what it was…"[25]

John Romans was the last witness before the court. He had spoken to George Crane on Saturday evening. Crane said, "he would soon die and in this case the innocent was a suffering [sic] in the place of the guilty, that he was dying for the protection of his wife."[26]

The testimony ended with a statement from Augustus Tapscott. "The prisoner after having been advised of his right to make his statement waived his right to make any statement."[27]

Alfred M. Carnes

Alfred M. Carnes (shown in some records and certainly in later life as Carns) was born June 13, 1822 in Tuscarawas County, Ohio to Manasseh Carns, Jr. and Elizabeth Sherrod.[28]

In the 1850 United States Census he is located in Bullitt County, Kentucky living with three other men. They all have the occupation of fanmakers.[29]

From 1850 to 1856 he is listed a Master Mason belonging to Salt River Lodge No. 180 in Bullitt County.[30]

Alfred married on Feb. 5th, 1852 in Nelson County, Kentucky. His wife, Maria Elizabeth, was the daughter of William Neill and Susanna Gray. The marriage took place at Cox's Creek Baptist Church in Nelson County.

Elizabeth's parents gave her and Alfred a house in Louisville, Kentucky in October of 1852. The couple sold this house in 1856. By that time they were living in Shelby County, Missouri. Their first child, Martha, was born there.[31]

Elizabeth had a brother, William B. Neill, who was living in Audrain County, Missouri. He had land in Prairie Township north of the present Scott's Corner. On the 4th of August 1858 Alfred bought 160 acres of land from Charles Benning and his wife, Nancy Jane for $1200.[32]

This parcel of land lay five miles north of Martinsburg. In 2009 terms it was on the west side of Highway 54, one mile north of Scott's Corner. It would have been wild prairie in 1858. Martinsburg would have been laid out only the year before.

By the 23rd of June the prisoner had been taken to Mexico. He was brought before Judge John P. Clark by Augustus Tapscott "on a charge of killing George W. Crane by shooting him with a pistol loaded with a leaden ball..."[33]

Bond was set at twelve hundred dollars. A. M. Carnes, Amos Ladd, Jacob Cartmell, Charles H. Benning, John E. Rossell, John C. Woodson, and John E. Hesket signed a security document acknowledging their indebtedness to the State of Missouri.[34] Carnes was told to appear before the November 1859 Term of the court. The name William B. Neill, Elizabeth's brother, appears in the body of the bond but he did not sign the document. On the same day, the 23rd of June, Alfred M. Carnes sold his farm to Amos Ladd[35] and J. W. Cartmell for $2000.[36] It is obvious that this was done to cover Alfred's bond.

The document no longer exists showing the events that took place at the November Term of the court. One can surmise, however, that a continuance was issued putting the case on the docket in the May 1860 Term.

Probate Law

Even as the criminal law investigations continued, probate law went into operation. The estate was being presented with various bills for payment.

On the sixth of July, Mary W. Crane renounced being administratrix of the estate in favor of George's brother, Joseph Crane, of Williamsburg.

Joseph set the date of 22 July 1859 for the sale of George's personal goods. Richard Childs was hired to call the sale for a two dollar and fifty cent fee.[37]

The negro boy, rented from the Coxes, had to be returned on the twelfth of July. Three dollars and fifty cents rental cost was paid.

On the sale day, 166 lots[38] were sold for the amount of $1,467.91. Justice Tapscott recorded the sale, listing item, buyer and amount.

Two notes were paid from the proceeds of the sale. One note dated 7 September 1858 was paid to Charles D. Crane, George's brother, in the amount of three hundred fifty dollars. A two hundred sixty-five dollar note was paid to Mrs. Doctor Graham.[39]

Spencer Davis was reimbursed six dollars for corn to feed the stock from the time of death to the day of the sale.

On August 3rd, 1859 a deed from Hugh A. Todd had to be recorded for a fee of seventy-five cents.

Not A True Bill

At the April 1860 Term of the Circuit Court, an Audrain County Grand Jury indictment was passed down. W. H. Hatch, Circuit Attorney, presented the case against Alfred M. Carnes. Mr. Carnes was indicted for murder. The offense charged was punishable by death.

At the May Term the Grand Jury returned the indictment, endorsed "Not a true bill." The defendant was discharged and the costs ordered to be certified for payment.[40]

The workings of the Grand Jury are secret. We do not have a document from which to assess why the indictment was not a true bill.

We can suppose with some justification that the jury must have felt that self-defense played an important role. The beating of Alfred M. Carnes by George W. Crane was severe. The jury could have felt that Carnes life was in jeopardy. The question of whether Thomas Crane had a pistol in his hand, though at first avoided, eventually ended with a witness saying yes. This, too, may have added to the jeopardy the jury must have considered.

Whatever story Carnes told, the Grand Jury must have believed him and they set him free.

By the time of the 1860 United States Census Alfred M. Carns and his family were settled in Dade County, Missouri.[41]

Missouri was dividing into two separate camps as civil war approached. The horrors of war were brought home to Alfred when he was captured as a civilian by bushwhackers. He was strung up and about to be hanged when he gave the Masonic distress signal. One of the bushwhackers was a Mason, who spoke up and saved his life.

This experience caused Alfred to join the 6th Missouri Cavalry (Union) on Aug 4, 1862. He served until July 19, 1865. During the war he suffered an injury to his eyes. By the time of his death he was blind.

In September of 1865 Alfred bought a farm in North Morgan Township of Dade County on Maze Creek just north of Bona. The road to Cane Hill crossed Maze Creek just below Alfred Carns' house. This crossing was known as Carns Ford.

Carns Ford is now under the waters of Stockton Lake. It still appears on geological maps and can be found on the Internet.

Alfred and Elizabeth raised a family of nine children. Elizabeth died January 27, 1894. Alfred M. Carns joined her in Long Cemetery, Dade County, Missouri on September 23, 1899.[42]

M. Y. Duncan, a Mexico lawyer of some repute, and in some cases disrepute, handled the probate paperwork. Occasional bills, such as one for August 8th, 1860, for five dollars for filing papers, were presented and paid. At one point he paid eight dollars and thirty-three cents land tax on 260 acres of Crane Estate land.[43]

Yearly reports were made on the estate and the guardianship of the children, Walter and Augusta Texas Crane.

On February 2, 1863 the notice of the final settlement of the estate was printed in the Missouri Telegraph newspaper, Fulton, by Joseph Crane, Administrator.

Guardianship continued for the children. On Mar. 20, 1866, Mary W. Crane wanted Fountain Vaughan to become guardian for Walter and Augusta Texas.[44]

Thomas, George's brother, who backed George in The Difficulty in the store died in 1870. He was buried in Liberty Cemetery.

His wife, Martha J. Crane, lived another thirty-one years dying in 1901. Martha maintained a large farm in southern Loutre Township.

A sad but interesting sidelight developed within this family. Thomas and Martha's youngest son was Charles T. Crane. Charles and his wife, Hattie, had a son, Charles Divers Crane.

Charles Divers Crane was the first Audrain County boy to die in World War One. He was with the 30th Infantry and was killed on the second day of the Franco-American offensive, which drove the Germans out of the Soissons-Rheims pocket. His death occurred on the 15th of July, 1918. He was brought back and reburied next to his parents at Liberty on August 1, 1921 with full military honors.[45]

Nathan Dix

Nathan Dix seems to have come to Audrain County sometime after the Civil War. He was from Brooklyn, Indiana. He married Mary W. Hays Crane. The place and date of this marriage has not been located. In 1870, however, this family unit was shown in the Census.[46] Augusta Texas and Walter are incorrectly listed with the surname Dix. This is an error. Their surname remained Crane, their father's surname.

Each year an annual settlement was made for the children. Judge G. B. MacFarlane handled the annual settlement for A. T. Crane in January 1873. By this time her guardian was Nathan Dix. In November of that year her final settlement took place at age sixteen. She received the sum of thirteen hundred nineteen dollars and seventy-four cents.[47]

June eighteenth, 1873, was the fourteenth anniversary of George's shooting. On that date Mamie Dix was born in Callaway County to Nathan and Mary Dix.[48]

Walter's final settlement is not found among the till papers. He would have turned sixteen in 1874. In 1875 Walter died on the twentieth of November. His stone lists his age as 18 when actually he was seventeen and would have been eighteen on the twenty-ninth of November. He was buried at Liberty Cemetery in Calla-way County. He lies next to his infant half-brother, Guy Otis Dix, who was born February twentieth, 1869 and died on August third of that year. Another infant of Nathan and Mary was buried nearby (no dates given).

Through the years Nathan always seems to have been called Capt. Dix. No reason has been found as to why he was given the Captain moniker. He does not appear to have served in the Civil War. Living on George's farm west of Martinsburg he was for many years the road overseer. Nathan may have been called Cap-tain for that reason or perhaps because he was for a time a Justice of the Peace in Loutre Township. He may have been called Cap-tain as an honorific for that position.

In February 1883 the Ledger attacked Capt. Dix saying the county court would not settle with him because of various impro-prieties as road overseer. The article was purely political and came about because Dix believed in the greenback reform platform. It was a very snide piece of work.[49]

Capt. Dix must have been popular, however, because by March the Ledger had to print a petition to the county court. It said in part "the undersigned petitioners, pray that you appoint Capt. N. Dix, as road overseer, west half of township 50, range 7…" It continued with a list of 65 residents who signed the petition. The Ledger concluded saying "the petition shows that Capt. Dix has made a good road overseer. The list contains the names of every man in his district except, perhaps, eight or ten."[50]

Augusta Texas Crane appears to have been a good manager. She, her mother, and Nathan extended ownership over the entire half section, 320 acres. She owned at least another 60 acres of land in the township. In Crigler's Addition to Martinsburg she owned Lot 7 in Block 2. In Original Martinsburg she owned a business lot. It was 40' X 60' on the southeast corner of Lot 3 in Block 13. In 1891 she paid $1700 for a house in Mexico's Block B, Hunter's Addition, east pt Lot 7 & all Lot 8, 420 E Promenade.[51] That house still exists today at Promenade and Trinity in Mexico. Augusta, her mother, Mary, Nathan Dix, and Mamie Dix lived there.

The year 1893 brought first sadness then joy to the household. On February 19th Mary W. Hays Crane Dix, wife of Nathan Dix died at age 55.[52] She was buried in Liberty Cemetery.

The joyous event was the marriage of Augusta Texas Crane and Thomas Jefferson Cornett on the 14th of June.[53]

April 3, 1896 saw the birth of their daughter, Charlotte (Lottie).

Mamie Dix had attended the Martinsburg schools and graduated

48

from Hardin College in Mexico. For many years she ran a boarding house at their Mexico address.

At age 50 December 4th, 1907 Augusta Cornett died suddenly.[54] She was buried at Elmwood Cemetery in Mexico. Her tombstone contains an incorrect birthdate. It says 1865, but should read 1857. When Mamie Dix's half-sister died Mamie assumed the raising of her niece, Lottie Cornett.

On March 17th, 1914 Capt. Nathan Dix died[55] and was buried at Liberty. He was 79. There is no marker on his grave.

Lottie Cornett attended Hardin College and graduated from St. Elizabeth's Convent in St. Louis. She became a fashion consultant for Marshall Fields and Co., Chicago. She worked for them for many years. She married R. M. Gelbach in Chicago on July 15, 1921. She visited Mexico frequently. Her father, T. J. Cornett died in 1923.[56] When Mamie Dix died in 1957,[57] Lottie, her husband being deceased, moved back to Mexico from Chicago.

In 1962 Lottie joined her parents and Mamie in Elmwood.[58] Since she had no children she was the last of the George W. and Mary W. Crane Dix line. The family had lived at 420 E. Promenade for seventy-one years.

Epilogue

The story after the story in this case is especially interesting. The author's fellow volunteers at the genealogical library in Mexico have always teased him about the possibilty of someone seeking information on a person he was researching. In this case it happened.

Roberta McReynolds, a teacher from Joplin, Missouri, contacted the library wanting to research Circuit Court Till #34 concerning Alfred M. Carnes. He was her great grandfather. It was a boon for the writer because she was able to provide valuable facts about Alfred's life after he was freed in Audrain County. It was information that the author needed to round out the tale and he was having trouble locating. It also showed that Alfred lived an honorable life after his Difficulty at Martinsburg. Thank you, Mrs. McReynolds, for making the full account possible.

Endnotes

[1]This farm lay to the south of modern day Highway U and east of Audrain Road 725. Its description is the NE ¼ of Section 21, Township 50N, Range 7W. The present day occupant is Jason Poindexter.

[2]"Probate Till of George Washington Crane, Jr.," d. 19 Jun 1859, No page nos. Audrain County, MO. Audrain County Probate Court, Audrain County Courthouse, Mexico, Audrain County,

Missouri. Hereinafter cited as Crane Probate Till.

[3]This land lying north of the George W. Crane Farm, was owned by Benjamin Y. Yates, a Kentuckian, who took up the land in Section 16 in 1856.

[4]"Testimony of Mary W. Crane," Given 21 Jun 1859. Audrain County, Missouri Circuit Court Tills, Till No. 34, Case No. 2, Case Files 1837-1883, p. 18. Audrain County Genealogical Society, 305 W. Jackson, Mexico, Audrain County, Missouri. Microfilm No. C37455. Hereinafter cited as Circuit Court Till #34.

[5]Circuit Court Till #34, p. 18.

[6]Circuit Court Till #34, p. 14.

[7]Circuit Court Till #34, p. 15.

[8]Circuit Court Till #34, p. 15.

[9]Circuit Court Till #34, p. 23.

[10]Circuit Court Till #34, p. 16.

[11]This store building was on the west side of Main Street in Martinsburg, MO. It fronted on Washington Street. The building no longer exists. Its rear entrance was on the alley north of the present day grocery store of Sandy Riutcel. The framing shop of Lisa Brandt now sits on the lot.

[12]A martingale is a heavy T-shaped piece of harness, it is a forked strap that prevents a horse from rearing its head. It connects the head gear with the belly band.

[13]Circuit Court Till #34, p. 5. William R. Martin's son, Caleb Tinsley Martin, ran the depot at that time and was also the town constable.

[14]Circuit Court Till #34, p.12. "Testimony of Dr. Burlington D. Brown."

[15]Crane Probate Till. Loose papers including the billing from Coil, French, and Company.

[16]Crane Probate Till. Loose papers including a bill from Brown and Noel.

[17]_____. History of Montgomery County, Missouri (St. Louis: National Historical Co., 1885), p. 590. Hereinafter cited as the History of Montgomery County, MO.

[18]Cemeteries of Montgomery County, MO. Compiled by the Montgomery County Clerk. Posted to a disk and donated to the Audrain County Genealogical Society.

[19]Circuit Court Till #34, p. 1.

[20]Circuit Court Till #34, pp. 1-5.

[21]Circuit Court Till #34, p. 4.

[22]Circuit Court Till #34, p. 8.

[23]Circuit Court Till #34, pp. 11,12.

[24]Circuit Court Till #34, p. 15. Alex was the son of Dr. Robert Graham, who settled and built a farm of 2500 acres at Mineola in

Montgomery County, MO. The doctor lent his name to Graham Cave, which was on his property. Alex married George's sister, Martha, on 10 Oct 1849.

[25]Circuit Court Till #34, p. 23. "Testimony of Morgan Collins."

[26]Circuit Court Till #34, p. 24. "Testimony of John Romans."

[27]Circuit Court Till #34, p. 24. "Statement of Augustus Tapscott."

[28]"Personal communications of Roberta McReynolds to Paul Hoer," 20 Sep 2009, Family Group Sheet of Alfred M. Carns, In personal files of Paul Hoer, 11320 Hwy 54, Laddonia, MO 63352. Hereinafter cited as Roberta McReynolds.

[29]1850 U. S. Census, Seventh Report, Bullitt County, Kentucky; p. 211b, National Archives Roll: M432_193.

[30]Roberta McReynolds.

[31]Roberta McReynolds.

[32]"Deed of Sale from Chas. H. Benning to A. M. Carnes," 4 Aug 1858 (Recorded 7 Aug 1858), Audrain County Deed Records, Book I, p. 170, Recorder's Office, Audrain County Courthouse, Mexico, Audrain County, MO. Hereinafter cited as Audrain Recorder's Office. Ronnie Arens owns this farm today.

[33]Circuit Court Till #34, no page nos., bond for A. M. Carnes.

[34]Circuit Court Till #34, no page nos., bond for A. M. Carnes.

[35]Future sheriff of Audrain County and founder of Laddonia, MO.

[36]Audrain Recorder's Office, "Deed of Sale from A. M. Carnes to Amos Ladd and J. W. Cartmell," 23 June 1859 (recorded 23 Jun 1859), Audrain County Deed Records, Book J, p. 436.

[37]Crane Probate Till. Loose papers including Richard Childs' bill.

[38]Crane Probate Till. Loose papers including the entire listing of sale items, buyers, and amounts kept by A. W. Tapscott.

[39]Mrs. Doctor Graham was Isabell Galbreath Graham. She was the wife of Doctor Robert Graham, not to be confused with her son, D. F. Graham, whose given name was Doctor. He was not an actual doctor.

[40]Circuit Court Till #34. A sheet showing Not A True Bill statement.

[41]1860 U. S. Census, Eighth Report, Dade County, MO; p. 143, National Archives Roll: M653_617. Family History Film: 803617. Alfred M. Carns, 37; Elizabeth, 25; William, 5; Martha, 3.

[42]Roberta McReynolds.

[43]Crane Probate Till. Loose papers including land tax payment.

[44]Crane Probate Till. Loose papers including guardian change.

[45]"Charles Divers Crane killed in France," Mexico Weekly Ledger (Mexico, Audrain County, MO), 8 Aug 1918, Thursday,

Vol. 60, No. 24, p. 1, col. 9. Hereinafter cited as Mexico Weekly Ledger.

[46]1870 U. S. Census, Ninth Report, Audrain County, MO; p. 506B, National Archives Roll: M593_756, Family History Film: 552255.

[47]Crane Probate Till. Loose papers including final settlement of Augusta Texas Crane.

[48]Death Certificate for Mamie Dix," 31 Oct 1957 (filed 7 Nov 1957), File No. 34736, The Division of Health of Missouri, Jefferson City, MO 65101. Copy in possession of writer. Although the Dix family lived in Audrain County, Mamie's death certificate shows she was born in Callaway County. It is possible that her mother was with her parents in Callaway County.

[49]Mexico Weekly Ledger, 15 Feb 1883, Vol. 24, No. 44, p. 2.

[50]Mexico Weekly Ledger, 8 Mar 1883, Vo. 24, No. 47, p. 2. List of Petitioners.

[51]Audrain County Assessment Book for 1892, ACAGS Library, Mexico-Audrain County Library, 305 West Jackson St., Mexico, Missouri 65265. Hereinafter cited as ACAGS Library.

[52]Mexico Weekly Ledger, 23 Feb 1893, Vol. 34, No. 47, p. 3.

[53]ACAGS Library, "Marriage of Augusta Crane and Thomas Jefferson Cornett," Audrain County, Missouri Marriages 1 Jan 1870-31 Dec 1899, Vol. 5, Audrain County Marriages, Book 3, p. 155.

[54]Mexico Weekly Ledger, 12 Dec 1907, Vol. XLIX, No. 40, p. 2.

[55]Mexico Weekly Ledger, 19 Mar 1914, Vol. LVI, No. 3, p. 1.

[56]Mexico Weekly Ledger, 15 Mar 1923, Vol. 65, No. 4, p. 3.

[57]"Death of Mamie Dix," Mexico Evening Ledger (Mexico, Audrain County, MO), 1 Nov 1957, Friday, Vol. 103.

[58]"Death of Lottie Cornett Gelbach," Mexico Evening Ledger (Mexico, Audrain County, MO), 27 Nov 1962, Tuesday, Vol. 108.

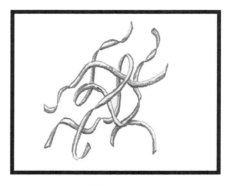

Thrums

Crumbs

U. S. Federal Census, 1860,
Slave Schedules for Loutre Township, Cuivre Township,
and Prairie Township, Audrain County, Missouri.

List of Slaveholders	No. of Slaves	No. of Slave Houses
John Fish	6	1
Wm. Dison	1	1
George Brown	3	1
John Coil	6	1
Sinclair Wilburn	4	1
Glover Collins	1	1
Coleman Brown	2	1
Masters Douglas	4	1
William S. Dishman	2	1
John T. Harrison	2	1
William B. Douglas	1	1
Jas. Harrison	6	1
Shelby Clark	2	1
George Thomas	1	1
William French	4	2
Wm. Morris	1	1
Laban Brown	1	1
William Martin	24	3

Loutre Township
     18 Slaveholders   71 Slaves
Cuivre Township
     37 Slaveholders   143 Slaves
Jerry Hall, largest slaveholder with 35 slaves, 4 slave houses
Prairie Township
     43 Slaveholders   166 Slaves
Rob. W. Sinclair, largest slave holder with 19 slaves, 4 slave houses

Note: Linn Township did not exist in 1860.

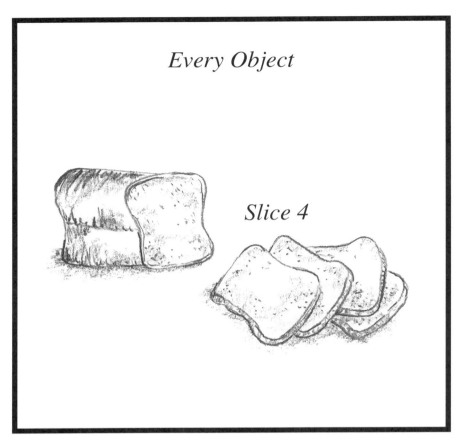

Every Object

Slice 4

The focus of this slice is a simple object, a plate. It is based on a common event, marriage. The tale is a bittersweet one covering long lives and everyday happenings. The narrative concludes with a mystery.

Bernard Adolph Fennewald (the Barney prominently mentioned in an earlier piece) and Elizabeth Hageboeck were married on the second of September, 1873.[1] They were both from Osage County and their wedding took place at St. Joseph Catholic Church, Westphalia, Missouri. He was the son of George Fennewald and his second wife, Margaret Hahn. She was the daughter of Francis Hageboeck and Elizabeth Kemna.

On the day after their marriage they packed up their belongings, including the plate pictured below (a wedding gift) and began their trek to the prairie at Martinsburg.

Wedding Gift Plate,
Courtesy of Don and Diane Schwartze, Martinsburg

There had been significant preparation for this day. Men of German extraction were raised with the idea of planning ahead. Oftentimes they worked for some years to build up a nest egg. They could then purchase a farm and support a wife and family.

Bernard, or Barney, wanted to learn the art of feeding cattle. He worked in St. Clair County, Illinois for a successful farmer engaged in this occupation. After some eight years, his knowledge enhanced, and with sufficient money, he purchased some prairie land in Audrain County. He envisioned fattening cattle on the lush grasses found there.

Barney bought one hundred and seventy acres of land from Jonas Kirback of Greene County, Illinois. He paid eight dollars and fifty-nine cents an acre for the land.[2]

With the move to Audrain County, Barney and Lizzie became true prairie pioneers. Prairie pioneers came a little later in the nineteenth century than the early pioneers. From about 1800 through the Civil War years, the early pioneers moved west and took up land. Roughly speaking, they came from the east coast and in a generation or two or three were in Virginia, Kentucky, Missouri, Oregon, and California. They avoided the flatlands and plains.

Prairies were bypassed for a variety of reasons. The Grand Prairie of Audrain County was little settled in the early wave. Those looking for land and homes chose locations near the rivers, like the Missouri, or streams, like the Loutre. It was here the first homesteaders were found.

Two changes had to happen before pioneers would take to the prairie. One of these was technological advance that made plowing prairie soils possible. A steel moldboard horse plow would scour and slide more easily down the furrow. The moldboard turned the grass upside down so that it would die. In 1837, John Deere began producng the steel plow. Eventually this improved technology began to have an effect on the plains.

The other change that was necessary was a mental shift in thinking. It was a common belief early that soil that would not grow trees was worthless. We now know that the prairie soils of the earth are where we find the breadbaskets of the world. Once that old idea began to crumble and the new idea gained credence, prairies became settled.

A St. Louis priest, Father Henry Muehlsiepen[3] (later Monsignor), preached to German Catholics living near the Missouri River. After the Civil War, the land there was filling up. Some moved farther south seeking farmland. Muehlsiepen became the second vicar-general to German Catholics for the Archdiocese of St. Louis. His sermons carried the message to farmers to move to the prairie at Martinsburg.

In 1886, when a new church was built at Martinsburg, it was dedicated by Vicar-General Henry Muehlsiepen. He was also instrumental in bringing the Sisters of the Most Precious Blood, founded in Guetweil, Baden, to the Archdiocese of St. Louis in 1872. They later centered in O'Fallon, Missouri in 1875.

Even though Barney and Lizzie were in the later group of pioneers, life was not easy. The wedding jouney by wagon to their Martinsburg farm led to a life together of more than 62 years. He built a successful business as a cattle feeder.

Barney's success on the prairie led others to come to Martinsburg. He provided a template to feeding cattle that others could emulate. His older half-brother, Joseph, and his wife, Mary (sister of Elizabeth) Fennewald also came to Audrain County and the Grand Prairie.

Elizabeth kept the home and raised the children. The first children were baptized at St. Brendan Parish, 10 miles west at Mexico, a 20-mile horseback ride. Later they helped to found St. Joseph Parish at Martinsburg.

Their eleven children were born at their prairie home. Their modest cabin was replaced with a substantial brick house in 1882. They lost an infant and a three-year-old son. A son, Joseph, aged 32, died of meningitis in 1910. A daughter, Johanna, wife of Henry Dubbert, drowned at age 31 in 1916. Frank, as stated in an earlier account, drowned in 1930.

George, Edward, Clara, Elizabeth, Mayme (later Deimeke), and Henrietta Schocklee survived their parents. Barney died in 1936. Lizzie died in 1937.

Barney's obituary in April, 1936 avers, "Possessed of a calm,

56

philosophical temperment, he has always been able to meet trials and sorrows that came to him in such a manner as only to deepen his strength of character..."[4]

When Elizabeth died, her obituary noted that she was the sole surviving founder of St. Joseph Catholic Church. She was one of the first officers of the St. Ann's Married Ladies Society at the church.[5]

Through it all the object of our interest was there. It was a re-minder of that wedding day, when two lives were joined and a prairie pioneer story was begun. Someone marked the plate with the special information so that it would not be forgotten. It was done so that the story this plate represents would not be lost. In study-ing the piece, one can see that it was displayed in a plate hanger for an extended period of time. The family was undoubtedly proud of this china.

The tale of the plate, however, ends in a mystery. No one can explain how this plate came to rest with the Schwartze family, who lived in the same community as the Fennewalds. Was there a sale, which took place after the passing of the elder Fennewalds? No one seems to know. The history ends in mystery, but it has been saved for you and the future.

Remember, every object has a history.

Endnotes

[1] _____. History of Audrain County, Missouri (St. Louis: National Historical Co., 1884), p. 565.

[2] "Warranty deed from Jonas Kirback to Barney Fennewald," 12 Dec 1871 (filed 14 Dec 1871, Audrain County Deed Records, Book U, p. 82, Recorder's Office, Audrain County Courthouse, Mexico, Audrain County, Missouri.

[3] _____. The History of the Archdiocese of St. Louis: A Condensed History of the Catholic Church in Missouri and St. Louis (St. Louis: Western Watchman Publishing Co., 1924), pp. 36, 45, 77, 95, 109.

[4] Martinsburg Monitor (Martinsburg, Audrain County, MO), 2 Apr 1936, Thursday, Vol. 17, No. 24, p. 1, col. 1. Hereinafter cited as the Monitor.

[5] Monitor, 17 Jun 1937, Vol. 18, No. 35, p. 1, col. 2.

Crumbs

Mexico Intelligencer (Mexico, Audrain County, MO), 24 Nov 1892, Thursday, Vol. XXI, No. 34, p. 6, col. 4.

Death of Adeline Nohrnberg

Adeline Nohrnberg, 17 years old, daughter of Chris Nohrnberg, died at Rush Hill, last Wednesday evening of typhoid fever. She had been attending school at the Clark Seminary and boarded at James Rosser's, where she died, being too ill to be removed to her home. She received every attention, however, and all that could be done was done to ward off the hand of death. Great sympathy is expressed for the girl's parents. The remains were interred at Laddonia.

Mexico Weekly Ledger (Mexico, Audrain County, MO), 18 Apr 1895, Thursday, Vol. XXXVII, No. 3, p.3, col. 7.

Closing Exercises of Collins Academy

The closing exercises of the second year of Collins Academy at Laddonia took place Thursday night at the Opera House. The evening was delightful, just cool enough to be pleasant. Early in the evening large crowds began to file into the building and by 8 0'clock, the time for the exercises to commence, the house was packed. The principal attraction of the evening was an elocutionary contest for first and second gold medals. The medals were handsome and appropriately engraved. The contestants were five young ladies, beautifully dressed in the very latest style. The programme rendered by the young ladies was most elaborate and contained many interesting features. Everyone who took part in it deserved great praise and credit. The exercises were under the direction of Mrs. Collins,[1] who is a graduate of Hardin College, and has had nineteen years of experience in teaching. She was principal of Clark Seminary at Rush Hill eights years and many regretted to see her leave. The contestants for the honors were Misses Josie Calhoun, Alice Moss, Jennie Clark, Ethel Darlington, and Edna Brown. After the rendition of the programme, three judges, having been selected from the audience before the exercises commenced without any previous notice, awarded first prize to Miss Jennie Clark, of Alton, Ill., and second to Miss Ethel Darlington, of Audrain.[2]

Laddonia is among the best little towns in the State, surrounded

58

by beautiful rolling prairies, occupied by wide awake, progressive farmers. The citizens of the town and vicinity are proud of their school and take a deep interest on the subject of education. While the public school is taught by good and competent teachers, Collins Academy is well patronized because it affords advantages that cannot be had at the public school.

[1]Mrs. Collins was Laura A. Collins, wife of Enoch A. Collins. Mr. Collins and Laura Clark were married 21 Jun 1893. She had gone to Harding College in Mexico, Missouri. At the time (1895) she had taught nineteen years, including eight years as principal of the Clark Seminary (nicknamed Miss Laura's Academy) in Rush Hill, Missouri. Enoch, known as Art, also taught at the Academy. Reminiscing in the Rush Hill Area, a 1981 Centennial Yearbook, states that the school was located on the west side of Center Street between 3rd and 4th. J. B. Clark, a local lumber dealer, established Clark's Seminary in a large frame house. By 1910 Art and Laura were teaching at Stephen's College, Columbia, Missouri.

[2]Ethel Darlington was the daughter of Rueben C. Darlington, whose farm, called Maple Grove Stock Farm, lay east of the land where Community R-VI Schools at Scott's Corner stands today. This farm was later owned by John Fennewald and is now operated as Becker Brothers. This is the farm where the graves of Jaeger and Sharp, hung by bushwhacker Alvin Cobb on July 18th, 1861 were found ten days later.

Mexico Weekly Ledger (Mexico, Audrain County, MO), 19 May 1887, Thursday, p. 3, col. 6.

MARTINSBURG MUSINGS
Mrs. Scott, Thomas Edwards, Chris Nohrenburg and Oscar Krieger left Wednesday for Europe; they were to be joined by others from Mexico and Wellsville. Oscar secured a passport from Washington before he left as he owes the Fatherland military service. Whodah

The Laddonia Herald (Laddonia, Audrain County, MO), 10 Jun 1915, Thursday, Vol. 31, No. 12, p.5, col. 1.

Ocie Dubray and sister, Miss Ruth, visited Perry Monday. Oci consulted Dr. Martin in regard to an afflicted mule.

Tax Assessment Book of Audrain Co., 1869,
ACAGS, 305 W. Jackson, Mexico, MO
Lot Owners in Martinsburg In 1869 (25 owners)

J. B. Clark
William R. Martin, Est. (Founder of Martinsburg, died 1867)
T. W. Haynes[Hanes] (Leatherworker in Slice 1)
C. T. Martin (Caleb Tinsley, son of William R. Martin)
M. A. Martin (Mary Ann, 2nd wife of William R. Martin)
George W. Twiner
C. C. Gantt (Chesley C., built brick store on lot 1, block 12)
Nimrod Smith
J. N. Haislip (James, had a store)
D. L. Thomas
Fletcher & Brother, Est. (Both killed trying to vote in 1868)
H. T. Clifton (Henry, blacksmith; wife ran a hotel)
D. Scannell (Dennis, N.MO RR section foreman, first house in town)
G. B. Leachman (George, had a store; also justice of the peace)
A. C. Hall (Alfred, preacher)
Thos. Smith
Edward Trabue
J. W. Crigler (John, real estate, Crigler Addition)
Joseph S. Muster (Carpenter, coffin maker, jack-of-all-trades)
Elizabeth Vaughn
William Nolen
Samuel V. Overbaugh [Overbagh] (had a store)
A. W. Tapscott (lumber dealer, justice of the peace)
W. H. Morris (William, property owner, farmer)
G. F. Rotsler (George, steam flour mill, burned 1872)

The Dalton

Slice 5

When we look at the Grand Prairie north of Martinsburg today, we see fine farms with big, productive fields of corn, soybeans, or other crops flourishing in a moderate climate.

If, however, we focus our minds back in time eight or ten thousand years, a very different picture emerges. There were people here, albeit, fewer in number. Small groups of paleo-Indians, hunter-gatherers, stalked the landscape in search of food and the necessities of life. Their ways of life, at that time, were named the Dalton Culture by archaeologists.

Philip Gastler recently plucked the Dalton point you see pictured below from the Grand Prairie soil. This chert or flint artifact is a tangible reminder of the men who walked here, long before us.

Dalton dart point found by Philip Gastler, Martinsburg

The picture shows a dart point. The quarter indicates the rela-tive size of the piece. It is part of a spear-throwing system utiliz-ing an atlatl. This arrangement was in use for thousands of years before the bow and arrow made its appearance.

Leverage is the key to the use of the atlatl. The atlatl is a shaft with a hook on the end. Sometimes the shaft may be grooved. This shaft held in the hand, possibly with a thong, lies back across the arm to the crook of the elbow. The butt of the spear is placed against the hook. At the end opposite the hook the shaft and spear are held in the hand. When it is thrown using the upper arm and wrist, the increased leverage allows a hard throw with an effec-tive distance of approximately thirty yards. Adding stone weights (called bannerstones) to the hook end of the throwing stick adds additional energy to the throw. Modern day hunters using the atlatl have successfully brought down deer in Missouri. They reported that it helps to be in a slightly elevated position. Small game may also be hunted with the tool.

An improvement on the technology was the use of foreshafts. Foreshafts were short wooden extensions fitted with a dart point. A hunter could carry several of these shorter foreshafts with a single six to eight foot long spearshaft. As needed, foreshafts could be added to the long shaft negating the necessity of carrying a number of these long cumbersome handles. An added incentive was the fact that a good, straight shaft, could be used over and over again because these shafts were difficult to make. One way of making a straight shaft was the use of an abrader. This stone tool was in two parts, with a half-groove on each piece. When the halves of this tool were positioned opposite each other around a potential shaft and moved back and forth, the result was a shaft smoothing pro-cess. It would make the shaft conform to a uniform shape. These people were highly skilled in making and using the tools they needed to survive and prosper successfully.

The lower portion of the chipped edge of the dart point was ground to dull it's sharpness so as not to cut the binding. The base was knapped lengthwise to thin it as an aid in hafting the stone.

The Dalton Culture was found in Central Missouri. It was named in honor of Missouri Supreme Court Judge S. P. Dalton of Jefferson City. He first gave information on the site to archaeologists.[1] Judge Dalton found the site named for him in a borrow pit along Highway 50-63 east of Jefferson City, where it crosses the Osage River. It was on a farm he owned there. It is on an old river terrace on the left bank of the river. Highway borrowing operations had removed eight feet of deposits above the site.[2]

This location is considered by archaeologists to be the type site for the Dalton Culture. These points and other tools (called an assemblage), however, are found in a wide area in the Mississippi Basin.

In the early 1950s the author excavated with the Missouri Archaeological Society at Graham Cave. It is found in Montgomery County, west of Danville, on the north side of Highway 70. The Dalton Culture was located in the lowest levels of Graham Cave. Radiocarbon dating shows an age of 6,000 to 8,000 B. C. E. or 8,000 to 10,000 years ago. The culture lasted for a considerable time.[3]

In this time period the one-mile-thick glacial ice sheet, which had flattened the prairie, had been retreating for thousands of years. The Ice Age megafauna of wooly mammoths, giant ground sloths, and ancient bison hunted by early man had died out. Gone were the Dire wolves and saber-toothed cats, which threatened the even older Clovis people. Many believe the Ice Age animals were driven to extinction by the Clovis hunters.

The environment was changing. The climate was still cold. It was almost like that found in mid-Canada today. The hunter tradition of the paleo-Indians was also changing. The hunter-gatherer way of life was beginning to develop. Roots, nuts, fruits, and small seeds were added to the diet. Deer and small animals were still very important. When it is cold, hunting provides the best sustenance. Foraging was gaining in providing food as people learned what items to include in their menu.

Camps were small and used for only a short time. Certain locations were no doubt used over and over. Caves and rock shelters were a good place to camp or winter over. Graham Cave at Danville and Arnold Research Cave at Portland were such places.

Bands were made up of a small number, an extended family or two. Perhaps this was twenty or so individuals. It has been estimated that at 8,000 B. C. E. Graham Cave could have had seventy-four individuals in residence based on size.[4]

Warm clothes were vital to the Dalton people. At Graham Cave, little bone needles with small eyes were found. Skins could be sewn together with these needles. Split-bone awls could be used to punch holes in leather. Bark moccasins were woven as well as ones made of animal skin. Ropes and mats were probably produced too.

Many objects used by the hunter-gatherers did not survive except in rare cases. Spear shafts, atlatls, tool handles, food containers, digging sticks, and animal traps were mostly made of wood. Arnold Research Cave, which was a very unusual, dry-as-dust cave, did preserve a foreshaft with its dart, some woven Juniper bark and skin moccasins, and lots of really old leaves, which had blown into the cave. In the open, none of these things lasted. We are left with stone points and tools, bone needles, awls, antler tools, and a few other items to study that have survived.

A drilled canine tooth was found with a burial at Graham Cave[5] indicating a ceremonial life. What has been called the Council Ring there is also believed to be part of the ceremonial trappings.

It is intensely interesting how these hunter-gatherers carried on their way of life for thousands of years, right here on the Grand Prairie and its edges. Can we consider them successful? We have been here 150 years or less. Do we have thousands of years ahead of us? Will we meet our challenges as they met theirs?

These are fascinating questions to ponder in the fading light of a summer's eve as we sit and watch night come on. Is that a skin clad hunter stalking a deer out there on the prairie?

Endnotes

[1]Robert E. Bell, Guide to the identification of certain American Indian Projectile Points (Norman: Oklahoma Anthropological Society, 1992), p. 18. Hereinafter cited as Guide.
[2]Carl H. Chapman, Archaeology of Missouri, I Columbia: University of Missouri, 1975), p. 97.
[3]Guide, p. 18.
[4]Ibid., pp. 96-97.
[5]Ibid., p. 96.

Crumbs

The Laddonia Herald (Laddonia, Audrain County, MO),
18 Jul 1918, Thursday, Vol. 34, No. 17, p. 2, col. 2.

SEEN IN THE CEMETERY

Take a walk through the cemetery alone and you will pass the resting place of a man who looked into the muzzle of a gun to see if it was loaded. A little further down the slope is a crank who tried to show how close he could stand to a moving train while it passed. In strolling about you will see the monument of the hired girl who tried to start a fire with kerosene and a grass covered knoll that covers the boy who tickled the mule's tail. That tall shaft over a man who blew out the gas casts a shadow over the boy who tried to get on a moving train. Side by side the pretty creature who always had her corset laced on the last hole and the intelligent idiot who rode a bicycle nine miles in ten minutes sleep unmolested. At repose is a doctor who took a dose of his own medicine. There with the top of a shoe box driven over his head is a rich man who married a young wife. Away over there reposes a boy who went fishing on Sunday and the woman who kept strychnine powders in the cupboard. The man who stood in front of the moving machine to oil the sickle is quiet now and rests beside the careless brakeman who fed himself to a 70-ton engine, and nearby may be seen the grave of the man who tried to whip the editor.

REMINISCING IN THE RUSH HILL AREA, CENTENNIAL YEARBOOK, 1981.

Many Americans, most of English descent, had difficulty with the spelling of names other than English, including those of Indian and French derivation.

By 1881, they were still having difficulties with names and it was agreed upon by Reusch and Hill (founders of Rush Hill) that they would anglicize the name to Rush Hill to get away from the German language pronounciation of Reusch. Also since the area was flat, prairie land with no hills within miles of the town, they would have their little private joke in naming it "hill," and so it was Rush Hill.

Martinsburg Monitor (Martinsburg, Audrain County, MO), 27 Jun 1935, Thursday, Vol. 16, No. 36, p. 3, col. 5.

TWO-HEADED CALF IS DRAWING CARD

The two-headed calf of which mention was made in an earlier edition of the Ledger, which was born on the farm of Edmond Kleinsorge, near Middletown, has been prepared and mounted by Edwin Seckler, amateur taxidermist, who lives just north of Martinsburg. The calf was dead at birth. It is of unusual size and the two heads and necks are perfectly normal. According to Mr. Seckler, it had two spines, one short spine joined the other near the hips. Mr. Seckler is a licensed taxidermist and has done some nice work in that line. The calf looks almost life-like, and approximately 50 people stopped at the Seckler home last week to see it.-Mexico Ledger.[1]

[1]This mounted calf is still in existence today.

Mexico Intelligencer (Mexico, Audrain County, MO), 8 Mar 1888, Thursday, Vol. 16, No. 48, p. 1, col. 6.

AGRICULTURAL WHEEL

A Society Established At Martinsburg

H. W. Hickman, president of the State Agricultural Wheel, and D. L. Langford of the Kentucky Wheel, arrived in the city Tuesday as previously announced, for the purpose of organizing a Wheel, an organization that is rapidly growing in Southeast Missouri. Mr. Langford made the opening address and briefly outlined the object of the order, which is chiefly for protection of the farmer.

The gentlemen were unsuccessful in securing the requisite number of names for an order here.

In Martinsburg 19 persons became members of the order and a lodge at once was established. The members are J. Martin, E. C. Wright, W. A. Cary, T. J. Lowder, A. J. Torreyson, Wm. Zjkan, Frank Ecker, D. R. Wright, George Canterbury, E. E. Miller, J. N. Johnson, Dennis O'Leary, James Madden, J. F. Burwell, J. R. Torreyson, S. L. Clements, P. S. Clements, S. T. Magrew, and Ross Clutter.

The Box Wagon Murder

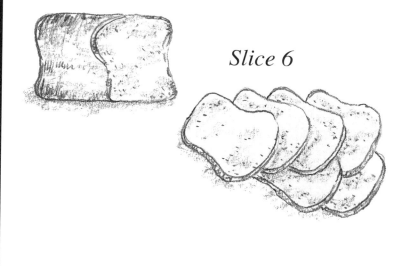

Slice 6

MONTROSE ATTORNEY'S VISIT RECALLS CRIME OF FIFTY YEARS AGO

M. B. Conrad, an attorney from Montrose, Mo., came to Martinsburg Monday seeking information of Bill Hartley and family, whom his records showed had lived in or near Martinsburg about fifty years ago. He was referred to Jacobi's Store and they found in their records that a Bill Hartley had lived at Martinsburg and traded at their store when they first came to town in 1885. They had no further information to give.

Fortunately, Mr. Charles Crane happened to be in the store and he recalled the man well. Mr. Hartley, he related, had killed a man by the name of Wiley [Wylie] fifty years ago. He was sentenced to the penitentiary for sixty years, the sentence later being made fifty years. During Governor David R. Francis' term he was pardoned and went to live in Henry County, according to Conrad. Last year he committed suicide, Conrad said, and when his family went to settle the estate they were informed that he had been married and had a family, when he lived at Martinsburg, before the murder. His wife divorced him after he was sentenced to the penitentiary. After his pardon he acquired another family and Mr. Conrad was employed to learn the particulars so the estate could be settled and the money go to the legal heirs.[1]

The foregoing article appeared in the Martinsburg Monitor in 1931. Our story begins in 1876. William Hartley was about to reveal a flaw in his 19-year-old character. We are not privy to the facts as to why he took the action he did. All we have are some scant circuit court records indicating that he was a volatile and violent individual.

A grand jury met in Audrain County, Missouri, in the October 1876 term of the circuit court. They determined that William Hartley

> "...did feloniously on purpose and of his malice aforethought make an assault in and upon one Cyrus Vanvacter and that the said William Hartley a certain shotgun then and being charged with gunpowder and leaden balls and then and there being a deadly weapon which said shotgun he the said William Hartley in both his hands then and there held then and there feloniously on purpose and of his malice aforethought did shoot off and discharge at the said Cyrus Vanvacter with the intent him the said Cyrus Vanvacter to kill against the peace and dignity of the state."[2]

Thus the story of William Hartley's destructive life begins.

William Hartley's father, Benjamin Hartley, coming from Greene County, Pennsylvania, had settled four miles south of present-day Benton City in Audrain County. His house was on forty acres in section 25. He owned another eighty acres immediately south in section 35.[3] Both sections were in Loutre Township. He arrived in Audrain County after the Civil War. All of his children were born in Pennsylvania. He had three boys and three girls with two different wives. His first wife, Dorothy, had died in the 1850s. William was the youngest, born in 1857, to Ben and Hannah Riley Hartley.

The two older sons, Leslie Carter Hartley and Levi Hartley were veterans of the Civil War. Leslie's record is tenuous. He is buried in Elmwood Cemetery[4] and is found in Precht's list of "Civil War Burials in Elmwood Cemetery." No record from Pennsylvania has been found. His brother, Levi, does have a record with the 46th Regiment, Pennsylvania Infantry. This regiment is well known and
68

fought in many important engagements. Levi, although he is buried in Elmwood,[5] is not found in Precht's list. The war was hard on Levi as we shall see later.

Another family venturing west to Audrain County was Cyrus Vanvacter, his wife, Sarah, and nine children.[6] They had come from Giles County, Virginia. Cyrus was certainly a renter or sharecropper, because tax records do not show him owning land. He is found living in Salt River, Prairie, and Wilson Townships at different times.

The Hartley and Vanvacter families became connected through two marriages. They may also have had an earlier connection. Sarah's maiden name was Leslie. Ben Hartley's first wife, Dorothy, had the maiden name of Leslie. That name was carried forward in the Hartley family in the person of Leslie C. Hartley. Sarah E. Hartley seems to have been named for Cyrus Vanvacter's wife, Sarah Leslie Vanvacter.

On 26 September 1868 Levi Hartley married Laura V. Vanvacter.[7] On 16 April 1870 Rodney Vanvacter, son of Cyrus, married Rebecca K. Hartley.[8]

From this we can gather that the shooting incident first mentioned was the result of some interfamily squabble. As was recounted, the grand jury met and indicted William Hartley for assault with intent to kill.[9]

On 9 October 1877, Sheriff Harrison Glascock of Audrain County delivered a subpoena naming Cyrus Vanvacter, Rodney Vanvacter, and James Harrison to appear for the State. He signed a document on October 10th stating, "William Hartley not found in Audrain County."[10]

Since he was not found in the county no further action appears to have been taken at that time. In those days if you were beyond the boundaries of the county, you were beyond the arm of the law.

There is evidence that William was hiding in Montgomery County. He must have returned to Audrain County in 1878. A sheriff's return shows that Sheriff Glascock executed a writ on the 15th of August 1878 by arresting and seizing the body of William Hartley and taking his body before Judge A. J. Douglas.[11] He was released on giving bond in the sum of five hundred dollars for his appearance at the October Term of the Circuit Court with Benjamin Hartley as security.[12] At this term of the court he must have gotten a continuance into 1879.

Another family that was added to the mix was that of Mastin Wylie. The name Wylie was found misspelled in historical and court records as Wiley. Wylie was a Missourian. He married an Indiana girl, Emeline Mitchell, in Scott County, Indiana on the 8th of November in 1848.[13] By 1850 he was in Ralls County, Missouri[14] and was still there in Spencer Township in 1860.[15] His family at that time consisted of one boy and four girls.

In 1878 he was in Loutre Township, Audrain County. He was renting land from Ben Hartley. He also borrowed money from Ben. His loan was for $35 dollars and his collateral for the loan was a box wagon.[16] The money was due on the first of January, 1879.

With the assault case hanging over him, William Hartley was married to Byra E. Barker on the 15th of December 1878.[17] She was the 19-year-old daughter of John and Nancy Barker of Upper Loutre Township, Montgomery County.[18] She was five months pregnant at the time of the marriage. This is the evidence of his laying low in Montgomery County. When she became pregnant, he escaped back to Audrain only to be arrested here. He went from the frying pan into the fire, so to speak. Cornered, he must have opted for marriage.

1878 had been a busy year for the Hartley's, including Leslie Carter Hartley. When the rest of the family moved west, Leslie had remained in Fayette County, Pennsylvania. He was a shoemaker and worked at his trade there. In April of 1878, he too came to Missouri and lived with his father until September 17th. He then went to work in George Hablutzel's Shoe Shop in Mexico. He worked there until the Friday before Christmas. At that time he went to spend the holidays at his father's house. William, his half-brother, was living there with his new wife.[19]

Events were quickly moving toward crisis by the first day of January, 1879.

Benjamin had given Leslie a note to present to Mrs. Mastin Wylie for payment. It was the note for $35 dollars given by her and her husband. About ten o'clock in the morning Mrs. Emeline Wylie came to the yard gate in front of Ben Hartley's house. Her daughter, Theodocia, was with her. Leslie went to the yard gate and told Mrs. Wylie the note was due. He told her he wanted the money. She replied, "You can't get your money. If you want your pay you will have to come and get the wagon."[20]

Leslie told her the wagon was to be delivered. She replied that, "Jimmy's (her son) busy hauling poles for Wagner and can't bring it down. If you want it," she said, "Come after it." Leslie answered, "We will come and get it, but that was not the contract."[21] Their conversation ended with nothing more being said.

William Jones, Ben's hired hand, and Ben and Levi Hartley witnessed the meeting at the gate. They were standing at the woodpile 50 or 60 feet from the gate. The woodpile was northeast of the gate and the house was 100 to 120 feet north of the gate.

Later in the afternoon, Mrs. Wylie again came up the lane with

Theodocia to the gate. She handed Leslie a letter sealed in an envelope directed to Ben Hartley. He took the letter to his father, but he would not accept it. Leslie put the letter in his pocket and kept it.[22]

In the evening of the first day of January 1879 Ben Hartley gave William and his wife, Byra, an infare dinner.[23]

Ben Hartley had a very small house, consisting of one room and a kitchen. He only had one extra bed. Leslie Hartley and William Jones gave up that bed to William and his wife. Leslie and William Jones walked a mile and a half south to the home of a neighbor, Henry Fielding Lowder.[24] Lowder lived on the Audrain-Callaway line. The two stayed with Lowder overnight until about eleven o'clock the next day. Then the two men began the cold walk back home.

When they were about a half-mile from Lowder's they met William on horseback. William wanted the Wylie note, which Leslie had in his pocket. William told Leslie to get on the horse and ride. He wanted to walk because he was nearly frozen.

When they got back to Ben's they harnessed the team of horses. Ben had asked his sons to go after the wagon. Leslie and William then set out to get the wagon at Wylie's. They rode the harnessed horses over to Wylie's, which was a little more than a quarter of a mile south from Ben's. It was a cold morning and they rode fast.

At the northwest corner of Wylie's yard the men stopped at the bars.[25] The bars were let down and they went into the lot to the wagon.

Leslie described his version of the events and they came very much into contention later. Leslie's version and that of the State varied substantially. His statement of the occurrences at Wylie's were given in a deposition taken at the Missouri State Penitentiary on the 15th of January 1880.[26]

William and Leslie turned the team around to hitch them to the wagon. The wagon was standing at the yard gate about thirty feet from the house. There were no doubletrees or neckyoke[27] on the wagon. The sideboards were leaning on the yard fence at the gate. About six or eight feet northwest was a sled with a pair of doubletrees and a neckyoke.

When they first rode up to the wagon, Mrs. Wylie and her son, James, came out of the west door of the house. Leslie told her they had come after the wagon. She said, "Yes."[28]

At this point the story differs. Mrs. Wylie's testimony was that when the Hartleys rode up, she went to the door and told them not to take the wagon unless they had the mortgage recorded. If it was recorded they could have it.[29] They agreed that Mrs. Wylie said, "There lays the sideboards on the fence."[30] William put them on the wagon. Leslie stated that James was with Mrs. Wylie. In her account he is in the house.

When the Hartleys started to take the doubletrees and neckyoke from the sled, they were told that those belonged to Mr. Harrison and that theirs were in the smokehouse. Leslie says he picked up the six-inch wide end gate to the wagon and he and William started for the smokehouse. Since the gate was frozen they stepped over the fence crossing.

Mrs. Wylie claims she came out of the house and picked up the top part of the endgate, six inches wide, one inch thick, and four feet long. She started to the house with it. She said, "Leslie jumped over the fence, overtook her, and with some violence took the board from her." She then ran toward the smokehouse. Leslie followed her with the board in his hand. When she reached the smokehouse, she turned around with her back to the door. Leslie slapped her once or twice.[31]

Leslie deposed, "Mrs. Wylie came up to me and asked to see the note. I had the endgate in my left hand and put my right hand in my pocket for the note. Mrs. Wylie jerked the board out of my hand and ran across the yard to the smokehouse. She threw the board down a little below the smokehouse."[32] William was inside the smokehouse when she turned her back against the door holding it to. He was trying to get William out of the smokehouse, but she had a stick against the door.

Leslie said in his deposition, "I did not slap or choke her. I tried to get hold of her to get her away from the door. She fought me off with the stick. I did not curse her then or at any time."[33]

When she got a little way from the door William got out with the doubletrees and neckyoke. James went to the south door of the house and called his father.

The Wylie's claimed that when William came into the yard he was near the kitchen door and met Mr. Wylie coming out. When Wylie saw Leslie choking his wife he called to his son, Jimmy and said, "Are you going to stand there and see your old mother abused in that way?" He yelled at William, "Get out of my yard!" That is when Hartley drew a knife in a threatening manner. Wylie picked up an axe that had been leaning against the house near him.[34]

The Hartley's counter argument was that when William was going toward the wagon, Wylie came out of the house, picked up the axe, and made at William with the axe drawn over his right shoulder in both hands. He said, "Goddamn you, I will kill you." He struck at William, and Hartley threw up the doubletrees and the axe struck them. They fell at Wylie's feet. William retreated down the path toward the garden.

Leslie shouted, "Run, Billy!" When William jumped the fence

72

he fell on the ice.

Wylie was getting over the fence with the axe raised and said aloud, "I've got you now."

Leslie picked up the endgate and ran to Wylie as he stood over William. He struck Wylie on the head with the endgate and he fell over the fence next to William. William got up and ran down in the garden. Wylie got up and chased after Leslie with the axe.[35]

The Wylie's testimony was that William got over the fence into the garden, Mr. Wylie stopped at the fence with his back to Leslie. Leslie ran up behind him and struck him with the board knocking him into the fence. Mrs. Wylie ran to help her husband up and back into the yard. William Hartley was standing in the garden.

Wylie started toward Leslie, who retreated across the fence into the horse lot. Wylie leaned against the fence facing Leslie. William jumped back into the yard and came up behind Wylie grabbing him around the neck with his left arm and raised his right arm holding a knife, with which he stabbed Wylie. He inflicted a wound just below the sternum. William dropped him and went into the horse lot.

Wylie turned to his son and said, "They have stabbed me." He walked to the kitchen door and as he reached out for the latch he fell prostrate. His wife and daughter dragged him into the kitchen. In about two minutes he was dead.

William and Leslie hitched up the wagon and one of them walked to the house throwing the mortgage into the door. The Hartleys drove off with the wagon.[36]

Leslie's retort was that Wylie chased him into the horse lot with the wagon. He called to William, "Come on and go home."

William replied, "Well, I will get my hat." He had lost his hat in the yard when he ran from Wylie. He picked up his hat and started toward the horses.

James Wylie was at the smokehouse and called to his father, "Here he comes, kill him." Then Mr. Wylie ran at William with the axe drawn.

William threw up his left arm and jumped back. The corner of the axe struck his arm. Wylie drew the axe again and William clinched with Wylie. Wylie was striking at him with the axe. William had his left arm around Wylie and ran his right hand in his pocket.

Mrs. Wylie hollered, "Kill him quick, he is getting out his knife."

Leslie saw the rough metal handle of a knife in William's hand. He closed the knife and put it in his pocket as he came through the fence.

Wylie put both hands upon his stomach and said, "My God, he

has got me killed at last." He started to the house.

James brought the doubletrees and neckyoke to the wagon, which was frozen in the ice. Leslie got the axe and chopped the wagon free, then put the axe on the woodpile. Leslie said he went to the west door of the house and gave the note to Mrs. Wylie. The Hartleys left, taking the wagon to their father.[37]

These were the arguments given later in court by the opposing sides.

When the Hartley's arrived at their father's house, William lay down on the bed. William's wife and his two sisters were over at John Clark's house, about a quarter of a mile away to the southeast. Ben Hartley, his wife, and William Jones were with William and Leslie. They finally decided that William, Ben, and Leslie would go over to John Clark's. Besides John Clark and his wife, William's wife and two sisters, there was another neighbor, George Wagner, who was in the house.

Leslie examined the wounds that William received. There was a cut on the back of his left arm between the elbow and shoulder, that went through two shirts and an overcoat. It was about an inch long. The holes in the shirts and overcoat corresponded to the wound on the arm. There was also a cut or bruise on the left side of his head, where the skin was broken and bleeding a little. Leslie thought it had been done with the pole of the axe.

They were at Clark's fifteen to thirty minutes, dressing William's wounds. When they left they did not tarry, but went over the steps and out of the yard in a hurry because it was a very cold day. The group went off to Ben's house to the northeast.[38]

Word was finally gotten to Sheriff Harrison Glascock about midnight that night. Despite the cold he left Mexico about 2 a.m. for the Hartley place. He arrested the boys while they were still in bed before daylight. They were in court for the preliminary hearing at 10 a.m. the next day.

On January ninth, the newspaper appeared with a screaming headline, "Heartless Hartleys! Two Blows From Behind – Cold Steel with a Warm Sheath – An 'End' Gate Sure Enough – Benton City the Scene of the Tragedy."[39]

Leslie Hartley, William's half-brother, was tried first. Many witnesses were called and deposed in Leslie's former home in Pennsylvania. All spoke favorably of him as a quiet, decent citizen and a good shoemaker.

J. Trimble and T. B. Buckner prosecuted the case. Leslie was defended by attorneys Forrist & Fry, with assistance given by D. H. McIntyre. On the 17th of December, 1879, the jury brought in a verdict of guilty of murder in the second degree. Leslie's penalty was assessed at ten years imprisonment in the state penitentiary.[40]

74

Photocopy of Leslie's Verdict

On December 19, 1879, Leslie Hartley called the Ledger before he boarded the evening train in the custody of Sheriff Glascock. They reported that he looked sad and pale. It was worse because he had to leave for prison just prior to the holidays, making it very difficult to leave home and friends for a life of confinement.

Prosecuting Attorney Trimble would not make a deal with William, who wanted to plead guilty for the same sentence. Trimble said, "Justice must take its course."[41]

The State presented the case that "the Hartley boys went to [Wylie's] get the wagon at all hazards; that they knew [Wylie] would not let them have it, and that they intended to take it by force or have blood, and they did both."[42]

Friends and neighbors from the area where Ben lived were called to be witnesses. The shopkeepers and others in the town of Martinsburg were subpoenaed to appear in court on one side or the other. The Vanvacters from the original charge of attempted murder were also on the witness list.

The State brought proved evidence that William had once said that "he would kill Wylie and make the hollows of that country flow with blood."[43]

William had an empty scabbard for a dirk in his pocket. He admitted that he had purchased a dirk from Mr. McKean[44] in October of 1878. He claimed he had lost it killing hogs before Christmas. He admitted stabbing Wylie with a pocket knife, not a dirk. William's testimony was rebutted by several of the State's witnesses.

75

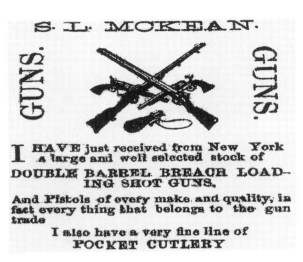

McKean's Ad in the Mexico Weekly Ledger

Dr. Taylor, from Martinsburg, testified that Wylie's death resulted from a knife wound. The blade had penetrated at least one inch into the apex of the heart. He determined this by a post mortem he held after disinterring the body of Wylie five days after it was buried.[45]

On the trial's last day, Hartley skipped his dinner. He sat pale and appeared to be in a trance. The jury foreman passed the verdict to the judge. The judge read, "guilty of murder in the second degree and sentenced to sixty years in the penitentiary."[46]

William did not move a muscle or show his feelings at all. He was to be assigned to work in the broom department. He did not think he would live out his sentence.

On March 15, 1880 William wrote a letter from the penitentiary. It was addressed to the Mr. R. M. White, the editor of the Mexico Weekly Ledger.

"Dear Sir: Yours of the 8th came duly to hand. I was delighted to hear from you. Words are inadequate to express my gratitude for your kindness in sending the Ledger to me. Eagerly read, I can assure you, not only by myself and brother, but by officers and others of this institution." He continues writing about a petition to Governor Phelps that was circulated in Walker Kilgore's (another murder case) behalf. William was mentioned in connection with the petition because he was given jail time and not the death penalty as Kilgore was. He takes exception to the malice shown him. He concludes his letter by saying, "I will say there are a great many upright, honest, and good citizens in Audrain County, but they are greatly in minority. Please excuse this, as I had to write it

76

in a hurry. I will do better next time. Please continue to send the Ledger. I remain Yours Respectfully, W. R. Hartley.

P. S. – We are kindly treated. Officers do all they can to make the prisoners comfortable. Leslie works in the shoe shop; I in the broom factory. Leslie and I cell together. Charley Parker is in the adjoining cell. W. R. H."[47]

Some parts of the letter Mr. White would not print because of objectionable personalities. He thought Hartley did not feel kindly toward the county people and jurors. He also thought the verdict could have been worse.

Emeline Wylie, Mastin's widow, moved to Montgomery County, Missouri following his murder. She still had four children living at home with her as shown in the U. S. Census of 1880.[48] By 1900, she appears to have been living in Wellsville with her daughter, Cora Hepler. Three of her six children are deceased.[49] In 1910 she is living with her granddaughter, Nona S. Gooch, wife of Ola T. Gooch, on the Martinsburg Road at Wellsville. She is 80 years old.[50] Emeline died on the 14th of March 1914, of senility and was buried in the Wellsville Cemetery.

William Hartley's brother, Levi Hartley, was admitted to the U. S. National Home for Disabled Volunteer Soldiers at Leavenworth, Kansas in 1889.[51] At age 47, his health had deteriorated due to the rigors of life in the field during the Civil War. He finally died of his afflictions in February of 1924. His body was brought back to Mexico and accompanied by his sister, Sarah E. Hartley, he was buried in Elmwood Cemetery.[52]

Byra Elizabeth Barker Hartley divorced William Hartley after he was convicted of murder. There is mystery surrounding what happened next. In the 1900 U. S. Census, Byra is shown as the wife of Leslie C. Hartley living in Mexico, Missouri. It states they were married in 1879 (she married William in December, 1878) and have been married for 21 years. Mabel, William and Byra's daughter, is shown as Leslie's niece, which is correct. She was 20 years old.[53] That figure is an obvious error. Mabel's death certificate avers she was born 12 April 1880.[54] Also an error. She was actually born 12 April 1879 and would have been 21 years old.

Whether this was accidental or intentional is anyone's guess. Since no marriage record can be found for Leslie and Byra, one is left to wonder if it was a common law marriage. The couple would have had to have been together before December, 1879 to make the 21 years of marriage work. Leslie left for prison at that point. It appears to be an incomprehensible muddle. Leslie died 10 January 1910 in Kansas City and he was buried in Elmwood Cemetery at Mexico. His death certificate makes no mention of Byra. In fact it shows his marital status as W for widowed. This was not the case.

The informant on the certificate, however, is E. A. McKinzie. He is the husband of Mabel Hartley McKinzie.[55]

Byra is shown living with the couple in the census of that year in Centralia, Missouri.[56] She is still living with them in 1920 along with her granddaughter, Byra McKinzie.[57] Byra died on September 14, 1926 and is buried at Liberty, Missouri, where the family was living in east Kansas City at the time.[58]

In 1888 David R. Francis was elected Governor of the State of Missouri. He was from St. Louis, Missouri. During his term in office one of his pet projects was prison reform.

At the end of his term, at a time when Leslie C. Hartley was completing his ten year sentence, Governor Francis pardoned William Hartley. Toward the end of February, 1890, both men were back in Mexico.

Home less than a week William was arrested and brought before J. J. Winscott, Justice of the Peace, for a felony. The Prosecuting Attorney J. R. Jesse stated that "William Hartley on the 24th day of February, 1890 did unlawfully, feloniously on purpose and of his malice aforethought assault one Benjamin Hartley with a deadly weapon. To wit one iron hammer with intent him the said Benjamin Hartley to kill..."[59] He was bound over to the grand jury.

The newspaper headlined: "IS HARTLEY INSANE? He Gets Into Trouble Again."[60] The Ledger stated, "Bill had made arrangements that day to go to St. Louis and get work in a broom factory. Some of the officers think Bill is crazy, judging from the way he cried and embraced his father and brother after having a fuss with them only a little while before."[61] Prosecuting Attorney Jesse believes if he is crazy he should go to Fulton. The paper continued, "Long confinement and family or financial trouble appears to weigh heavily on Hartley's mind and it is hard to tell at this writing whether he is crazy or not."[62]

On March 12, 1890 William was released from jail on recognizance. Leslie and Sarah Hartley put up five hundred dollars each to obtain his release until the grand jury action was taken on June 3, 1890. On that day E. L. Grigsby, foreman of the grand jury, returned a finding of "not a true bill."[63] William Hartley was once again free.

Levi Hartley and Laura Vanvacter Hartley were living in Clinton, Henry County, Missouri in 1880.[64] The couple had adopted a girl, Mattie Hartley, who had been born in Scotland. When Levi entered the Disabled Soldier's Home in 1889, it is uncertain what happened to Laura and Mattie.

Following William's episode after returning from prison, he, too, went to Henry County. In 1895 he married a widow, Laura F. Hatch Boyd, who was born in Illinois in 1855. She was married

78

to John A. Boyd and they lived in Henry County, Missouri. He died in 1888 there and was interred in Bear Creek Cemetery. They had four children, three of whom were living in 1900.[65] Admarian Boyd, John A. Boyd, Jr., and Mary Ethel Boyd.

The situation became more convoluted when Ethel married Joe Hartley. Joe Hartley was the son of Oscar Hartley and had been born in Iowa. One source says he was a nephew of William.[66] It is more likely he was a cousin, but no connection can be found. This is, no doubt, how William or Bill, as he was known in Henry County, met Ethel's mother and led to their eventual marriage.

In 1885 Ben Hartley sold his 160-acre farm, 4 miles south of Benton City, to Leslie C., Syntha [Cynthia], Maria, and Sarah E. Hartley for $3,500.[67] He moved to Mexico. Hannah Riley Hartley, his second wife, died in 1888. Ben then lived with his daughter, Sarah, in the southeast part of town. In 1898 he died at the age of 85. In a funeral conducted from Sarah's house, he was buried beside Hannah in Elmwood Cemetery.[68] Later, Sarah also moved to Henry County.

Sometime between 1900 and 1910 Rodney and Rebecca Hartley Vanvacter, along with their son, Leslie Minor Vanvacter, moved from Audrain County to Henry County.

In December 1910, Laura died of Bright's disease, at the age of 57. She was laid to rest beside her first husband in Bear Creek Cemetery.[69] Around 1923 Bill moved in with Joe Hartley. He lived there about eight years. In November 1890, he began living with Joe's daughter, Ethel Wolford, wife of Ralph Wolford. A week and a half later he committed suicide by shooting himself with a .30-.75 Springfield rifle.

He had given ample evidence that he was contemplating his own demise. He went into the Lennartz Furniture and Undertaking Company on Friday to see caskets. He picked one and said, "that one is good enough for me."[70] When he left he shook Mr. Lennartz's hand and said, "Goodbye Frank, this is the last time you will see Bill Hartley alive."[71] Next, Bill went to Claud Elliston at his hardware store. He had Claud draw up a new will. When Frank Lennartz heard this he called Mr. Wolford. Wolford told him he knew of Bill's desire and was trying to reason with him. He understood Bill was upset and acting irrationally.

On Saturday Ethel asked Bill to bring the milk cow in from the pasture. While she was milking the cow she heard the report of a gun. Investigating she found Bill at the mouth of a small cave about 12 feet from the house. He was dead.[72] On Sunday afternoon his funeral took place at Bear Creek Cemetery. It was a dramatic end to a dramatic life.

M. B. Conrad, an attorney, travelled to Martinsburg to find

Bill's former family, Byra and Mabel, to settle the estate.

Bear Creek Cemetery received in order Rodney Vanvactor (1927), Rebecca Vanvactor (1931), Leslie Minor Vanvacter (1945), Ethel Boyd Hartley (1953), and Joe Hartley (1955).[73] Sarah E. Hartley died in 1939 and was taken to Elmwood Cemetery in Mexico, Missouri[74]

The Clark family, who had lived nearby and had been his friends and neighbors, eventually owned Ben Hartley's farmland. That land is still owned by an ancestor of the Clark family, William Clark Ford.

Endnotes

[1]Martinsburg Monitor (Martinsburg, Audrain County, MO), 30 Apr 1931, Thursday, Vol. 12, No. 24, p. 1, col. 5.

[2]Audrain County Circuit Court Tills, Till #722, Case No. 24, Case Files 1850-1911, no page numbers. Audrain County Area Genealogical Society, 305 West Jackson Street, Mexico, Audrain County, Missouri. Microfilm No. C55976. Hereinafter cited as Circuit Court Till #722,

[3]_____. Historical Atlas of Audrain County, Missouri (Philadelphia: Edwards Brothers of Missouri, 1877), p. 25. Hereinafter cited as 1877 Atlas of Audrain.

[4]"Grave of Leslie Hartley," Elmwood Cemetery, Block A, Lot 27, West Liberty Street, Mexico, Audrain County, Missouri.

[5]"Grave of Levi Hartley," Elmwood Cemetery, Block A, Lot 27, West Liberty Street, Mexico, Audrain County, Missouri. Hereinafter cited as Grave of Levi Hartley.

[6]1860 U. S. Census, Giles County, Virginia; p. 857, National Archives Roll: M653_1345; Family History Film: 805345.

[7]"Marriage Record of Levi Hartley and Laura Vanvacter," 26 Sept 1868, Audrain County Marriages, Recorder's Office, Book B, p. 128, Audrain County Courthouse, Mexico, Audrain County, Missouri. Hereinafter cited as Audrain County Marriages.

[8]"Marriage Record of Rodney Vanvacter and Rebecca Hartley," 16 Apr 1870, Marriage Records of Callaway County 1821-1871, Ada Ferguson, compiler and publisher, Fulton, MO. Audrain County Area Genealogical Society, 305 West Jackson Street, Mexico, Audrain County, Missouri.

[9]"Indictment of William Hartley," 15 Aug 1877, Circuit Court Till #722, no page numbers.

[10]"Arrest Warrant for William R. Hartley," 10 Oct 1877, Circuit Court Till #722, no page numbers.

[11]"Sheriff's Return, Arrest Warrant for William R. Hartley," 15 Oct 1878, Circuit Court Till #722, no page numbers. Judge A. J. Douglas was a neighbor of Ben Hartley's. He had a large farm

about one and one-half miles northeast of Ben.

[12]"Sheriff's Return, Recognizance Bond for William R. Hartley," 15 Aug 1878, Circuit Court Till #722, no page numbers.

[13]"Wiley [Wylie] – Marriage," 8 Nov 1848, Ancestry.com. *Indiana Marriage Collection, 1800-1941* [database on-line]. Provo, UT, USA: Ancestry.com Operations Inc., 2005. Family History Library, Salt Lake City, UT, OS page 1305346.

[14]1850 U. S. Census, District 73, Ralls County, Missouri; p. 177B, National Archives Roll: M132_411.

[15]1860 U. S. Census, Ralls County, Missouri; p. 636, National Archives Roll: M653_642; Family History Film: 803642.

[16]_____. History of Audrain County, Missouri (St. Louis: National Historical Co., 1884), p. 260. Hereinafter cited as History of Audrain.

[17]"Marriage Record of William Hartley and Byra Barker," 15 Dec 1878, Audrain County Marriages, Book B, p. 352.

[18]1870 U. S. Census, Montgomery County, Missouri; p. 130B, National Archives Roll: M593_794; Family History Film: 552293.

[19]"Leslie Carter Hartley's Deposition," deposed 15 Jan 1880, Missouri State Penitentiary, Circuit Court Till #722, no page numbers. Hereinafter cited as Leslie's Deposition, Circuit Court Till #722.

[20]"Leslie's Deposition," Circuit Court Till #722, no page numbers.

[21]"Leslie's Deposition," Circuit Court Till #722, no page numbers.

[22]"Leslie's Deposition," Circuit Court Till #722, no page numbers.

[23]infare dinner: a reception or party given a newly married couple.

[24]1877 Atlas of Audrain, p. 25.

[25]bars: a gate or barrier in a fence consisting of poles placed horizontally across the opening.

[26]"Leslie's Deposition," Circuit Court Till #722, no page numbers.

[27]doubletree: a pivoted pole with a whiffletree attached to each end, used in harnessing horses two abreast.
neckyoke: a pole hooked at the front and below the horses neck between the pair with a central ring attached, through which the tongue of the wagon is placed.

[28]"Leslie's Deposition," Circuit Court Till #722, no page numbers.

[29]History of Audrain, p. 260.

[30]Mexico Weekly Ledger (Mexico, Audrain County, Mis-

souri),19 Feb 1880, Thursday, Vol. 21, No. 44, p. 3, cols. 3,4.

[31]History of Audrain, p. 260.

[32]"Leslie's Deposition," Circuit Court Till #722, no page numbers.

[33]"Leslie's Deposition," Circuit Court Till #722, no page numbers.

[34]Mexico Weekly Ledger, 19 Feb 1880, Vol. 21, No. 44, p. 3, cols. 3,4.

[35]"Leslie's Deposition," Circuit Court Till #722, no page numbers.

[36]Mexico Weekly Ledger, 19 Feb 1880, Vol. 21, No. 44, p. 3, cols. 3,4.

[37]"Leslie's Deposition," Circuit Court Till #722, no page numbers.

[38]"Leslie's Deposition," Circuit Court Till #722, no page numbers.

[39]Mexico Weekly Ledger, 9 Jan 1879, Vol. 20, No. 38, p. 3, col. 2.

[40]Mexico Weekly Ledger, 18 Dec 1879, Vol. 21, No. 35, p. 3, col. 3.

[41]Mexico Weekly Ledger, 25 Dec 1879, Vol 21, No. 36, p. 3, col. 2.

[42]History of Audrain, p. 261.

[43]History of Audrain, p. 261.

[44]History of Audrain, p. 262.

[45]Mexico Weekly Ledger, 9 Jan 1879, Vol. 20, No. 38, p. 3, col. 3.

[46]History of Audrain, p. 263.

[47]Mexico Weekly Ledger, 25 Mar 1880, Vol. 21, No. 49, p. 4, col. 1.

[48]1880 U. S. Census, District 114, Montgomery County, Missouri; p. 167B, National Archives Roll: 705; Family History Film: 1254705.

[49]1900 U. S. Census, District 70, Montgomery County, Missouri; p. 9A, National Archives Roll:T623_876.

[50]1910 U. S. Census, District 109, Montgomery County, Missouri; p. 10B, National Archives Roll: T624_800; Family History Film: 1374813.

[51]"Levi Hartley's Admittance," 1889, Ancestry.com. *U. S. National Homes for Disabled Volunteer Soldiers, 1866-1938* [database on-line]. Provo, UT, USA: Ancestry.com Operations Inc., 2007.

[52]"Grave of Levi Hartley, Block A, Lot 27, Elmwood.

[53]1900 U. S. Census, District 12, Audrain County, Missouri; p. 15B, National Archives Roll: T623_837.

[54]"Death Certificate for Mabel McKinzie," 8 Jul 1938, (filed 11 Jul 1938), File No. 21638, The Division of Health of Missouri, Jefferson City, Missouri 65101.

[55]"Death Certificate for Leslie Hartley," 20 Jan 1910, (filed 22 Jan 1910), File No. 507, The Division of Health of Missouri, Jefferson City, Missouri 65101.

[56]1910 U. S. Census, District 9, Boone County, Missouri; p. 7A, National Archives Roll: T624_770; Family History Film: 1374783.

[57]1920 U. S. Census, District 56, Geary County, Kansas; p. 20A, National Archives Roll: T625_533.

[58]"Death Certificate for Byra Hartley," 14 Sep 1926, (filed 10 Jan 1927), File No. 28226, The Division of Health of Missouri, Jefferson City, Missouri 65101.

[59]"Arrest Warrant for William Hartley," 24 Feb 1890, Audrain County Circuit Court Tills, Till #541, Case No. 4, Case Files 1865-1898, no page numbers. Audrain County Area Genealogical Society, 305 West Jackson Street, Mexico, Audrain County, Missouri. Microfilm No. C42278. Hereinafter cited as Circuit Court Till #541.

[60]Mexico Weekly Ledger, 27 Feb 1890, Vol. 31, No. 47, p. 3, col. 2.

[61]Mexico Weekly Ledger, 27 Feb 1890.

[62]Mexico Weekly Ledger, 27 Feb 1890.

[63]"Not a True Bill Return," Circuit Court Till #541, no page numbers.

[64]1880 U. S. Census, District 173, Henry County, Missouri; p. 353B, National Archives Roll: 689; Family History Film: 1254689.

[65]1900 U. S. Census, District 73, Henry County, Missouri; p. 6B, National Archives Roll: T623_858.

[66]The Montrose Tidings (Montrose, Henry County, Missouri), 20 Nov 1930, Thursday, Vol. 14, No. 42, p. 1, col. 2. Hereinafter cited as The Montrose Tidings.

[67]Mexico Intelligencer (Mexico, Audrain County, Missouri), 26 Nov 1885, Thursday, Vol. 14, No. 34, p. 3, col. 3.

[68]"Grave of Benjamin Hartley," Elmwood Cemetery, Block A, Lot 27, West Liberty Street, Mexico, Audrain County, Missouri.

[69]"Grave of Laura F. Hartley," Bear Creek Cemetery, 611 SW751 Rd., Henry County, Missouri.

[70]The Montrose Tidings, 20 Nov 1930.

[71]The Montrose Tidings, 20 Nov 1930.

[72]The Montrose Tidings, 20 Nov 1930.

[73]"Vanvacter and Hartley Graves," Bear Creek Cemetery, 611 SW751 Rd., Henry County, Missouri.

[74]"Grave of Sarah Hartley," Elmwood Cemetery, Block A, Lot 27, West Liberty Street, Mexico, Audrain County, Missouri.

Crumbs

Mexico Weekly Ledger (Mexico, Audrain County, MO),
20 Mar 1890, Thursday, Vol. XXXI, No. 50, p. 1, col. 3.
An Incident of 1862,
Wherein Some of Krekel's Command Figured Conspicuously

Correspondence of the Ledger.
Laddonia, Mo., March 13

Twenty-eight years ago the 17th of March, three promising
young men were killed near here. In 1862 Capt. Alf Payne and
Judge Underwood were organizing two companies for the Confederate army near Madisonville in Ralls County. The measles broke
out and several sick men were sent home, Young Smith, Mercer
Hoffman and Will Jackson being of that number. When they arrived near where Judge Grigsby now lives[1] they were halted by Lt.
Hubert, of Krekel's gang,[2] who demanded of them where they were
going. The boys replied, "Sick soldiers going home." Ordering
his command to surround them Hubert told them plainly he would
have to kill them. Telling them to dismount, Smith and Jackson
obeyed. Hoffman inquired if they were going to shoot them like
dogs, at the same time saying, "I will save myself if I can." He
spurred his horse swiftly over the prairie, followed by Lt. Hubert,
with pistol in hand, firing as he pursued. They run half a mile
before a shot took effect. Hoffman, thinking he had distanced
his pursuer, turned in his saddle to look back when a shot struck
him near the eye, dismounting him. Smith and Bill Jackson stood
their ground and died facing their captors. A militia man (I could
call his name)[3] put a pistol under Jackson's chin and fired, the ball
coming out at the top of his head and killing him instantly. Smith
was shot in the forehead and killed. They then ran a saber through
his body after he was dead. The dead bodies of the boys were left
where they fell. The federals then went to Russell Wells' house
and told him what they had done, ordering Wells to hitch up his
wagon, go after Hoffman and bring him to the house. He was still
alive. Wells was then told to send for Dr. Alex Crawford, who

84

would not come, he thinking it was a plan to take his life. Dr. A. F. Brown was then called, who arrived at 2 o'clock, p.m., and examined the dying boy. There was no chance for him to live and in a few moments he was dead. They then arrested J. W. Hoffman, father of young Hoffman, Jno. J. Sutter, Jno. J. Smith, father of Young Smith, and Nick Smith, brother of the dead boy, and "Uncle" Billy Wells and took them to Wellsville and put them in prison for having boys who wanted to go to the Confederate army.

OLD RESIDENT

[1]In 1890 Judge Grigsby lived several miles northeast of Laddonia.

[2]The Wells farm was about a mile southwest of where Grigsby lived.

Martinsburg Monitor (Martinsburg, Audrain County, MO),
2 Feb 1933, Thursday, Vol. 14, No. 15, p. 1, col. 6.

BELIEVED ALLEDGED SPURIOUS MONEY
WAS MADE HERE
The belief that alleged spurious 50 cent pieces had been made and probably circulated in Mexico, Columbia, Jefferson City, and other nearby cities, as well as in Fulton, was expressed Wednesday by United States Marshal Russell Daniel of Kansas City at Fulton, it was learned from the Fulton Gazette. Mr. Daniel arrested Bill Debo and Cliff Myers of Callaway and took them to Jefferson City Wednesday on charges of circulating spurious money. It was expected he would soon be in Mexico for investigation.-Mexico Intelligencer.

Mexico Weekly Ledger (Mexico, Audrain County, MO),
16 Jan 1890, Thursday, Vol. 31, No. 41, p. 3, col. 6.

Martinsburg Matters
Our new paper, the Message, is a nice little sheet for the size of our town. Our editor seems to be a nice gentleman and he has a nice lady for a wife. We hope they may prosper in our little village

85

and that our citizens may patronize his paper.

Miss Minnie Romans leaves for Indiana the 18th of this month, where she will attend school.

Mexico Weekly Ledger (Mexico, Audrain County, MO),
13 Feb 1890, Thursday, Vol. 31, No. 45, p. 1, col. 7.

Married at Last

Rush Hill, Mo., Feb 7.-For a long while young Thomas McDermott, of Martinsburg, and Miss Minnie Romans, of the same place, but who has been attending Clark Seminary at Rush Hill, have wanted to get married. They escaped and came to Mexico and obtained a license Dec. 20th. The irate father[1] appeared on the scenes and prevented the marriage, although they were both of age.

Sometime since, the young lady expressed a desire to attend school at Rush Hill. She did so and last Thursday a friend of McDermott drove up to the boarding place of Miss Romans with the statement that her father had sent for her. She entered the buggy and was driven to the nearest Justice of the Peace. They are now married and visiting relatives in Hallsville.

[1]The irate father was George P. Romans. He died at 73 in 1913. He lived his last two years with his daughter, Mrs. Thos. McDermott in Wellsville.

Tax Assessment Book of Audrain Co., 1882,
ACAGS, 305 W. Jackson, Mexico, MO

Lot owners of Reusch-Hill [later Rush Hill]

All lots are owned by Gustave Reusch or by Reusch & Hill.

Lot owners of Benton City

J. B. Armistead
Louis Barker
Saml. Barker

The Big Barn

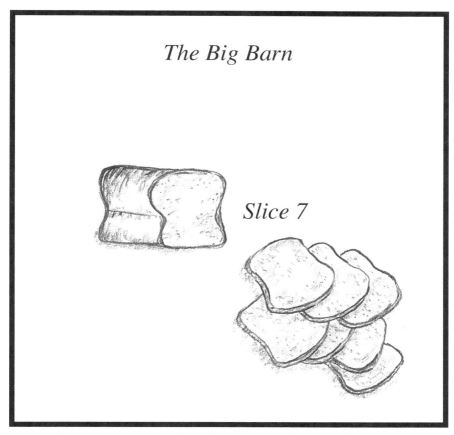

Slice 7

In the past it was called the largest barn in Audrain County. Is it still? The writer doesn't know, but when one peers into its cavernous interior, the only thought that comes to mind is yes, this has to be the largest barn in the county.

The barn is one hundred feet wide and ninety and a half feet long, an area of 9,050 sq. feet. It is three stories tall. Atop the roof are two huge cupolas with their lightning rods pointing into the sky.

On either side of the central passage on the ground floor are two sizeable granaries. Each one would hold thousands of bushels of ear corn. At the north end of this hallway and at the end of each granary is a wooden silo, three stories tall and inside the barn itself. The silos are thirty six feet tall from the ground level to the top plus four feet buried in the ground. They stand in excellent shape.

When a person climbs the ladder up through the center of the barn, you are ascending next to an elevator, perhaps two to three feet square. It starts at the ground on the east side of the main hallway and proceeds upwards nearly to the peak of the barn. When the climber reaches the second loft the elevator continues on and towers over him. At the top a series of pipes could be attached to the elevator and the grain directed to various parts of the barn. The tops of the granaries are open at this level. An individual looking down into the granaries begins to realize how vast they are. It is as though one were looking into the hold of a cargo ship. The granaries are cross-braced with a series of steel rods to help the walls support the weight of the grain.

On the second story lofts, hay could be stored and thrown down the outside to racks on the ground floor below, where the animals could eat it. On the outside of each granary were troughs where grain could be fed to the animals.

In traversing the barn from west to east, each component would appear in the following manner. The west wall made up the back of the hayrack, with the slats sloping up to the second story hay loft. Next, a large open space provided an area where animals could shelter and feed. There are support posts here to hold the weight of the upper stories. Attached to the outside wall of the granary were troughs, where grain could be fed to the livestock. The next part was the granary itself. The central hallway allowed the teams and wagons to bring grain into the elevator and the silos.

The east wall and barn was a mirror image of the west side, the granary with its troughs, the open area with its posts, and the east wall hay rack. It presents itself as a beautiful design for feeding large numbers of livestock.

In its day, cattle were fed to weights of 1200 to 1400 pounds. Mules were being fed out as meat animals during this period around the First World War. Mule flesh was popular, especially in cities like St. Louis. Weighty hogs were also being produced. The big barn was one that feeders at the beginning of the twentieth century would dream about.

Ruben Pew Brown and Alice Moomaw Brown

The man who took the dream and made it a reality was Ruben Pew Brown and his wife, Alice Moomaw Brown.[1] The newspapers reported constantly on Ruben's activities.

"Ruben brought in 125 nice shoats from Laddonia. Ruben shipped two carloads of 1250 pound steers. Ruben was feeding 200 cattle. Ruben was feeding 180 hogs."[2] Ruben P. Brown was busy. His brother, William J. "Jack" Brown,[3] was located on a nearby farm and he too, was a busy feeder. Jack's place was the original Brown farm here. A third brother, Charles, had also come to Audrain County. Sometime later he moved on to settle in Nebraska.

The three brothers were born in Montgomery County, sons of G. W. "Wash" Brown, who had come to Missouri from North Carolina. Wash Brown married Frances Pew[4] and farmed north of Bellflower. When the brothers came to Audrain County they set up operations six miles north of Rush Hill in Audrain County, when they were able to purchase land. This was in the West Lick neighborhood named for West Lick Creek, which ran on the east side of Ruben's farm and through part of Jack's farm.

One brother, George, remained in Montgomery County. He farmed the home place. Another brother, James H., lived in East St. Louis, Illinois and St. Louis, Missouri.[5] He worked for the Illinois Central Railroad.

Two unmarried sisters, Misses Mollie and Birdie Brown, eventually lived on one of Ruben's farms. It was one mile to the west of the barn.

The Moomaw family were early pioneers of Audrain County. Joel Moomaw, Barry, Illinois and Susan Pence, Eaton, Ohio, were Alice's parents.[6] The Moomaw Cemetery was on the west bank of West Lick Creek east of Rube's farm. The Moomaw farm was east of West Lick Creek and Ruben's place.

No one seems to know just when the barn was built. Although a thorough search has not uncovered the information, there are clues. One is a newspaper report of damage done to Rube's "mammoth" barn by two consecutive storms in June of 1915.[7] The building had obviously been built before then. Frances Schooler, a granddaughter of Ruben and Alice's, tells this family story. "The summer of the year the barn was built, my dad (Lee Sonwalt) told me he and "Bird", Ruben's sister, moved the lumber and nails by wagon loads from the railroad at Rush Hill. Lee was the youngest of three Sonwalt boys and was often excluded from farm work with his father and two older brothers. He was left home to take care of his two younger sisters. He said he was glad to go to work for wages and get out of housework."[8] If Lee was twelve or thirteen at the time, it would put the date around 1913 or 1914. A newspaper search has not turned up any corroborating evidence.

Prior to 1915 the work on the building began. Five train carloads of cypress lumber and a carload of nails were placed on the siding at Rush Hill. Horses and wagon moved the materials to the site six miles north. When the nail kegs were empty a team and wagon was dispatched to Rush Hill. The kegs would be refilled from the train car and brought back to the construction site.

Ruben Brown's Big Barn – Front View

It surely must have taken a considerable time to construct such a huge structure. It is amazing that no hint of news can be found about such a major project in a rural area. It's design is consistent with the cutting edge agricultural ideas of the time. Wooden silos were being advertised in the newspapers, particularly by the La-Crosse Lumber Company.

Later concrete silos began to appear.

Mollie Brown died in 1915 at age 56. She was buried at Littleby Baptist Church.[9]

Through the teens Brown's heavy steers topped the markets. In 1916, for example, three carloads of heavyweights averaging 1441 pounds brought $9.55 in St. Louis.[10]

In January of 1917 James Brown was killed in an accident on the train he was conducting. He had worked for the Illinois Central for 20 years. He was buried in Belleville, Illinois. George, Jack, Rube, and Birdie attended the funeral.

Ruben and Alice had two daughters, Fannie (born 1901) and Fern (born 1907). On December 22, 1920, Fannie married Lee Sonwalt.[11] As a wedding gift Ruben transferred five hundred acres of farmland to the them. This became a Missouri Century Farm in 2006. The farmhouse and 280 acres is owned by Frances Schooler and 220 acres is owned by her sister, Ruby Hale.

Ruben Pew Brown suffered from Bright's disease and died at 62 on March 7, 1924.[12]

Across the road southeast was a farm owned by Sterling Price Dubray. His son, Cefalis "Fal" Paul Dubray, married Ruben's younger daughter, Fern, in 1927.[13] He received the other half of
90

Ruben's property. Alice moved to Laddonia.

In 1932 Fal purchased the land of J. T. "Bud" Anderson. It was across the road south from the big barn. A fair sized barn still stands on this ground. Fal was a farmer and feeder.

On May 28, 1940, Frances Ann "Birdie" Brown, who had resided at the Fulton State Hospital for a couple of years, died of pneumonia. She was nearly 70 years old.[14]

In August 1952 Fal Paul Dubray drowned in a pond near the big barn, while seining for fish with four neighbors. He could not swim. When he slipped on a steep underwater bank, he went under and could not be saved. He was 47 years old, survived by his wife and two daughters. He also left two sisters, Mrs. Ruth Stotler and Mrs. Joe Beagles; three brothers, Frank, Ocie, and Glenn.[15]

Alice Brown lived to be nearly ninety years old, dying in 1953.[16] Both she and Ruben are buried in the Laddonia Cemetery.

Fannie Brown Sonwalt died in 1969. She had been a member of Littleby Baptist Church. Lee died in 1995 and they are buried in East Lawn Cemetery, Mexico.[17]

Fal Dubray and Fern Brown Dubray are also buried in East Lawn.[18] Fern died in 1967. She had remarried and her tombstone reads Fern Playter.

Today, the wisdom of Ruben's use of cypress lumber is evident. The structure is well-preserved and although appearing abandoned, it stands strong as though waiting for the next string of cattle to be fattened. It is painted white and has a good sheet metal roof to carry it into its next hundred years.

Endnotes

[1] _____. History of Audrain County, Missouri An Update 1936-1986 Audrain County Historical Society, 501 S. Muldrow St., Mexico, MO. Hereinafter cited as History of Audrain Update.

[2] The Laddonia Herald (Laddonia, Audrain County, Missouri), 31 Jan 1918, Thursday, Vol. 33, No. 45, p. 4, col. 3. Hereinafter cited as The Herald.

[3] 1900 U. S. Census, District 7, Audrain County, Missouri; p. 12A, National Archives Roll: T623_837.

[4] 1880 U. S. Census, District 108, Montgomery County, Missouri; p. 5B, National Archives Roll: 705; Family History Film: 1254705.

[5] The Herald, 25 Jan. 1917, Vol. 32, No. 45, p. 1, cols. 4,5.

[6] "Death Certificate for Alice Brown," 14 Mar 1953, (filed 16 Mar 1953), File No. 8692, The Division of Health of Missouri, Jefferson City, MO 65101.

[7] The Herald, 24 Jun 1915, Vol. 31, No. 14, p. 4, col. 4.

[8] "Oral Interview with Frances Schooler," 22 May 2011, by the

author, 11320 Hwy 54, Laddonia, MO 63352.

[9]The Herald, 11 Nov 1915, Vol. 31, No. 34, p. 1, col. 6.

[10]The Herald, 18 May 1916, Vol. 32, No. 10, p. 3, col. 5.

[11]History of Audrain Update, p. 419.

[12]"Death Certificate for Ruben Brown," 7 Mar 1924, (filed 8 Mar 1924), File No. 6716, The Division of Health of Missouri, Jefferson City, MO 65101.

[13]History of Audrain Update, p. 521.

[14]"Death Certificate for Frances Brown," 28 May 1940, (filed 29 May 1940), File No. 18036, The Division of Health of Missouri, Jefferson City, MO 65101.

[15]Mexico Weekly Ledger (Mexico, Audrain County, MO), 28 Aug 1952, Thursday, Vo. 94, No. 3, p. 1, cols. 1, 2.

[16]History of Audrain Update, p. 519.

[17]Headstone inscription for Lee and Fannie Sonwalt, East Lawn Memorial Park, Section 2 Forest Lawn, Lot 41, Mexico, Missouri. Author's visit 30 May 2011.

[18]Headstone inscription for Fal Dubray and Fern Dubray Playter, East Lawn Memorial Park, Section 2 Evergreen, Lot 167, Mexico, Missouri. Author's visit 30 May 2011.

Crumbs

Mexico Weekly Ledger (Mexico, Audrain County, MO), 24 June 1924, Thursday, Vol. 66, No. 23, p. 2, col. 5.

MRS. GROVER WEBER FEEDS TRAMP WITH SHOT GUN BY SIDE

Last week Mrs. Grover Weber entertained a stranger in her home in a very unusual manner. While preparing the refreshments she carried a double barrel shot gun with her, although too scared to use it. But here is how she came to do this.

One day last week Mrs. Weber was called on the telephone by a neighbor telling her a bad looking tramp was coming. She huriedly ran upstairs and waited until she thought he had departed and then went to sewing. Soon she heard someone walking in the rooms downstairs and she knew it wasn't her husband as he was in an oat field three miles away. She finally gathered courage, and walked to [the] top of the steps and inquired of this tramp what he wanted. He replied work, then thinking to scare him she asked why he didn't go to the barn and see the men. He sarcastically replied he knew there were no men around, and commanded her to come on downstairs and get him something to eat.

She came down with the shot gun and gave him something to eat. He remained two hours, taking leave just before her husband arrived. Needless to say Mrs. Weber doesn't care to entertain this way again. –Laddonia Herald.

Mexico Intelligencer (Mexico, Audrain County, MO), 28 Jan 1886, Thursday, Vol. 14, No. 43, p. 1, col. 4.

MANGLED MEN

The enterprising little town of Rush Hill on the C. & A. Railroad, 10 miles northeast of this city, was the scene of terrible accident Friday, intelligence of which reached this city at night, but not until the next morning were the shuddering details known –told to a representative of the INTELLIGENCER by one who waited on the mangled men during the night. It is well known to the readers of this paper that parties at Rush Hill have been vigorously boring for coal for some time past and that flattering progress has been made with the work. It was in this mine situated about a quarter of a mile from town that the accident occurred.

W. T. Lott, Jr., took the contract to sink a shaft 300 feet. He employed Uzzell and Foree to do the work. The work would have been completed in a short time, as a depth of 94 feet and 8 inches had been reached. No evidence of coal, even at this depth, had been apparent.

The men had put in a blast and were going on with the tamping process. The supposition is that a spark flew from the tamping rod and ignited the powder and an explosion followed.

The names of the injured men are Robert Foree and Lewis Uzzell, the latter now lying in critical condition. Foree was frightfully burned about the head and abdomen and its thought he will lose one of his eyes. Uzzell had both arms and one leg broken.[1]

[1]Both men survived. Uzzell lived his life in Rush Hill. He was badly crippled.

93

The Hoer's Horses

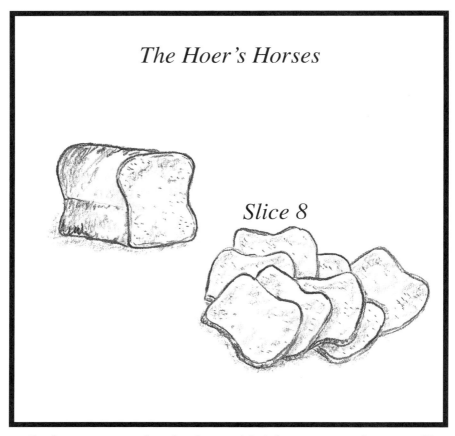

Slice 8

In times past, work animals provided the power on farms to till the soil and do all of the other chores required of them, making farming possible. Oxen, horses, and mules broke the prairie sod under extreme conditions. Added to this was the job of transporting the family hither and yon, to church, dance, or shopping.

Pioneers all mention two scourges that attended plowing and made life miserable for man and beast no matter what job was undertaken. Those hardships were green-headed flies (a small horse-fly) and prairie rattlesnakes.

Harness was improved by making a crosshatch of strings attached to the harness and draped over the animal's body. As the animal moved the strings would also move and keep the flies from landing and biting. Besides the animals, the man behind the plow was also attacked. Many times farmers worked by moonlight to avoid the flies.

Snakes were a problem day or night. They tended to gravitate to the furrow that the work animal generally followed. To help protect the animal, the legs were wrapped with burlap to prevent a strike from hitting home.

Travelling in cold weather was always a hardship. Horseback riders often dismounted in the cold and led their horses, walking to warm themselves up. Leo Hoer, son of Martin Hoer, told of cold trips to church when chickens would be sacked and placed on the floor of the buggy. Feet were placed among the chickens and blankets wrapped around the body and over the chickens to provide warmth. Leo also told the following story about an evening's entertainment.

Lawrence Fennewald and Rose Barron were married in 1917 and moved to take up housekeeping on a farm about five miles north from Shadowlawn, where Leo lived, toward Rush Hill. It was decided by a group of young people, relatives and friends, to go to Lawrence's for a chivaree or charivari. This was a visit to put on a mock serenade of singing, yelling, tin pans, horns, and general noisiness outside the home of a newly married couple.

They gathered on a cold winter evening for the trip. The team was harnessed and hitched to a box wagon. Everyone climbed aboard and off they went.

The chivaree went as planned with plenty of noise and laughter. It was Lawrence and his bride's duty to invite the harassing crowd into the house for refreshments. It was a pleasant evening with a good time had by all. That is, until the merrymakers had to go out into the freezing cold night and get into the wagon for the trip home in the chill moonlight.

The gang covered themselves with blankets, and once Leo got the team going he climbed down into the bed of the wagon, too. They pulled blankets up to their chins and sang as the wagon bounced and jounced along. The driverless team trotted on through the night back to Shadowlawn. They found their own way back down the road by which they had come.

With his family, shucking corn into a box wagon one freezing day, the writer was standing on the rear of the load. The upper layer of ground was frozen and mud lay beneath, so the wheels of the loaded wagon kept breaking through the crust. The horses struggled, and each time the wagon wheels sank, they would throw their shoulders into the harness. This produced a jerk. At the unexpected jerk, the writer tumbled off the back of the wagon and cracked his head on the frozen ground. This may account for his strange actions today.

Horse associations were common at this time. Martinsburg had a buggy horse association. People bought shares in the association, which provided buggy horses for its members. Margaret Torreyson, a pioneer schoolteacher, had shares in the Martinsburg Buggy

Horse Association.

Another organization that had been around for some time was the Anti-Horsethief Association, a vigilance committee designed to catch horse thieves. It first developed in Kansas prior to the Civil War and was very effective in preventing theft or in catching thieves who did steal horses.

One community member, who was remembered for his work with the Anti-Horsethief Association, was Captain W. T. Lott. He lived in various areas of Audrain, and his Captain moniker came from his leadership position in the Association. At 85 he died and was buried at Liberty Cemetery.

At Shadowlawn, the farm of Martin Hoer in Loutre Township of Audrain County, Missouri, draft animals were the backbone of the work force. Big, powerful horses were a prize to be desired. Percheron's were one breed of these horses.

In March of 1913, Martin Hoer, his half-brother, George Kersting, and brother-in-law, Joseph Linneman, joined together with other local farmers August Bertels, William Riutcel, George Lail, Frank Seckler, Casper Aulbur, Henry Stuckenschneider, and Joseph Dubbert in forming the Martinsburg Percheron Horse Association.[1]

This group purchased a fine black thoroughbred Percheron horse from an Association at Greeley, Iowa. He was four years old, weighed over 1900 pounds, and cost the Martinsburgers eighteen hundred dollars.

The Percheron was named Sultan, and his registry number was 55653. An ad in the Audrain County Oracle said, "Sultan is a fine black Percheron Draft Stallion with a small star in forehead. He is 4 years old, 16 ½ hands high and weighs between 1900 and 2000 pounds and has fine action and good disposition. He is of the well known Brilliant stock. The horse shows for himself."[2] The ad listed an extensive pedigree for Sultan.

Sultan was put out to stud by the Martinsburg Association at Shadowlawn, the Martin Hoer farm, 1 mile north and 2 miles west and four miles east of Benton City. Fifteen dollars insured a living colt. The next year he was put to stud at George Kersting's farm near Martinsburg.[3]

SULTAN 55653

SULTAN, the Black Percheron Draft Stallion owned by the Martinsburg Percheron Horse Association will make the season at the Geo. Kersting farm ¼ mile North-east of Martinsburg.

TERMS

\$12.50 to insure living colt,

Martinsburg Percheron Horse Association

Sultan's Ad in the Audrain County Oracle

Percherons were the most numerous draft breed in the United States by 1915.

Many times, Leo Hoer related the story of an event he witnessed while watching Sultan one day.

Sultan was walking across the barn lot. Ahead of him a flock of pullets were scratching and picking in the dirt. At Sultan's approach most of the chickens fled, but a few, intent on their gleaning, stayed. As Sultan stepped forward, Leo saw the hoof come down on a pullet. He immediately envisioned death and destruction. Instantly the hoof lifted and out ran the pullet unharmed.

A horse's hoof has a cavity behind the actual nail. Sultan's hoof was so huge, a foot across, that with the additional lift of a horseshoe, it provided a space in which the chicken survived.

Clement, Martin's youngest son, was always a lover of horses. He was particularly fond of palominos of which he owned several in his life. He spoke lovingly of a team of Martin's, a wonderfully matched set of draft horses. They were two peas in a pod. These horses were turned out of the barn on a cold winter's day to be watered and allowed to exercise. Clem chopped the ice in the water tank so that the team could drink. When they finished they trotted off toward the pasture stirring the snow which lay on the ground several inches deep. It was bitter cold, ten below zero, as the team playfully nipped at each other and increased their pace from a trot to a gallop. Clem watched as they sped off into the pasture and raced full speed to the farthest end of it. As the team turned one of the horses stumbled, went to his knees, and fell heavily in the snow.

Clem quickly went to the end of the field. When he arrived he found that the horse was dead. It was surmised that the cold drink of water along with the vigorous exercise had precipitated a heart attack. To break such a matched pair, even to death, was very painful.

Clem retrieved his skinning knives from the house and dressing warmly he went into the cold pasture and skinned the dead animal. That tanned hide was a covering over a couch in the family home for many, many years. He had horses on the farm into his eighties.

One of the most amazing, unusual, yet true situations that developed concerning the Hoer horses occurred when Martin Hoer sold one of his horses to a man living in southern Illinois.

At the appointed time the horse was led to Martinsburg and put aboard a train bound for East St. Louis, Illinois. Once there, the horse was loaded onto another train for the trip south. Arriving in southern Illinois the buyer claimed the horse and took him home to his farm.

Life went on at Shadowlawn as usual for a couple of weeks.

Then one morning when Martin left the house to do his morning chores, he heard a whinny at the front gate. When he investigated, there stood the horse he had sent to Illinois. The family was dumbfounded as to how this horse could have found his way home, swimming two major rivers.

Contacting the buyer, he related that he had had the horse at his farm for two days. Then the horse disappeared and the man, with the help from his neighbors, could not find him.

The purchase price was returned to the buyer. The loyalty of this horse was rewarded by his being allowed to remain at Shadowlawn.

As the Hoer children grew older and became more active in farming, more teams were needed. To outfit the additional teams, U. S. Army surplus harness was purchased. Brass tipped hames and the brass "U.S." buttons of World War I army harness were evidence of the prior owners.

Brass US Button from WW I Harness
Courtesy Digger Dan's Antiques

Harnessing horses was a time consuming task. More teams meant even more time harnessing them. David Rankin (1825-1910) was called Missouri's Corn King. He had land at Tarkio in Atchinson County, Missouri. Working with horses (lots of them) he farmed 25,000 acres. He raised 1,000,000 bushels of corn for feeding 12,000 cattle and 25,000 hogs. It is said that it took three hours in the morning (starting at 3 a. m.) and three hours in the evening just to harness and unharness the horses with a large cadre of farmhands. The amount of time harnessing and the amount of land it took to feed the horses made steam engines and later, gasoline tractors, very attractive to farmers.

A barn at Shadowlawn built in 1904 had a large portion set

aside for horses. These areas had hay racks designed so hay could be dropped down into them from the loft above. The horses could then eat the hay by inserting their heads between parallel bars of wood vertically set and leaning outward. The wooden dividers were brightly polished at the point where the horses had rubbed against them again and again over the years.

A step-grandson of Clem's has since destroyed the barn. The barn was unusual in that the wood had been floated down the Mississippi River from the north to Lousiana, Missouri. One could see where the mortises and tenons had held the lumber together on its trip downriver. From the LaCrosse Lumber Company in Louisiana, it was hauled by wagon to Shadowlawn. Leo reported that when he went to school in the morning the neighbors were gathering to work on the barn. When he came home in the evening, the framework was all up and pegged.

The barn is only a memory now and the hundred twenty years of memories of Hoer horses at Shadowlawn are also fading fast.

Endnotes

[1]Audrain County Oracle (Martinsburg, Audrain County, MO), 20 Mar 1913, Thursday, Vol. 6, No. 19, p. 1, col. 6. Hereinafter cited as The Oracle.
[2]The Oracle, 17 Apr 1913, Vol. 6, No. 23, p. 4, cols. 3,4.
[3]The Oracle, 28 May 1914, Vol. 7, No. 28, p. 8, cols. 3,4.

Crumbs

Martinsburg Monitor (Martinsburg, Audrain County, Missouri), 24 Jul 1930, Thursday, Vol. 11, No. 37, p. 1, col. 6.

Magnet Truck to Clear Gravel Roads of Metal
Stretch from Martinsburg to No. 40 gives up
over 100 pounds, proves scrappiest road.

Picking up 35 pounds of miscellaneous metal per mile, the State Highway Department's maintenance truck found the gravel road from Martinsburg to 40 the worst they have had in some time. The truck bears three powerful magnets, each weighing 900 pounds, which took up nails, bolts, spikes, and all scrap metal along the highway.

The truck picked up a total of 100 pounds of scrap on the road from Martinsburg to 40. Highway 54 from Farber to Scott's Corner yielded 125 pounds to the three magnets.

All gravel highways around Mexico will be covered by the machine while it is working in this section. It will work out of Mexico to Vandalia, Centralia, and Paris, on highways 54, 22, and 15.-Mexico Intelligencer.

It is no wonder that Martinsburg yielded the most scrap as all trucks from North Missouri to St. Louis are routed through here. The highway from Mexico to New Florence should be concrete.

Mexico Intelligencer (Mexico, Audrain County, MO), 22 Mar 1888, Thursday, Vol. 16, No. 50, p. 1, col. 3.

Small But Sufficient
Audrain Adopts the Local Option Law by Ninety-four Majority
Full returns from the Local Option election show a majority of 94 for the law. The contest was conducted in a quiet, dignified manner throughout and there is very little bad blood over the result. The anti-license people are naturally elated over the outcome and it is quite likely that they will move for a submission of the question in Mexico within a short time. Following are the majorities by precincts:

DRY		WET	
Mexico	27	Molino	17
Vandalia	13	Edwards	8
Black	25	Beagles	30
Farber	69	Martinsburg	50
Laddonia	16	Benton City	71
Crows	55	Canada's	24
Rush Hill	3		___
Friendship	14		200
Gant	19		
Rowena	16		
Naylor	37		
	___		
	294		

Scott's Corner & Highway History

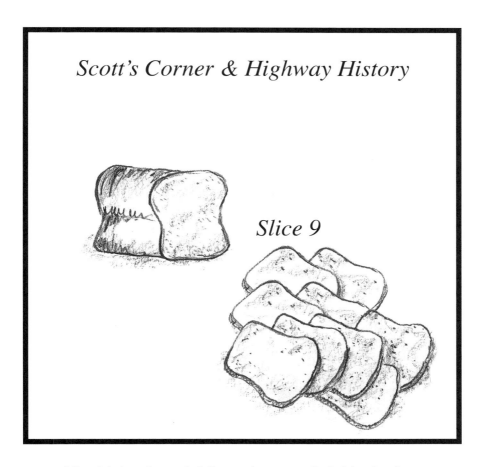

Slice 9

"On driving through Missouri enroute [to] this city from Pueblo, a motorist in approaching Mexico by an indirect route from the east, came at last to 'Scott's Corner.' This stranger to the state had heard these words over and over in Colorado and again and again in Missouri. Finally as he approached Mexico he noticed sign posts, heard [an] increasing number of directions given from 'Scott's Corner,' and at last was able to put death to his own curiosity and ignorance by actually seeing the place which is familiar through the entire land to tourists. He feels greatly relieved that he had viewed this historic branch of roads, and is feeling completely initiated as a real Missourian, since he, too, can say that he turned a certain direction at 'Scott's Corner'; four miles north of Martinsburg.

The trail to discovery would have been very nerve wracking had the tourist not been upon a wedding journey and in unusually high spirits throughout the search."[1]

Even in 1927, Scott's Corner was important in the minds of the traveling public. This article emphasizes that belief.

Corners, the intersections of roads, have been important throughout history. Directions were given, distances measured and locations confirmed by using corners. Across the land corners were and are significant in people's lives. Great cities and small towns grew up around many of these geographical spots. Many more are locally important.

Baysinger Corner, Rice's Corner, and many others are found in Audrain County. The most famous corner, however, is Scott's Corner. At Scott's Corner, U. S. Highway 54 running east from Mexico intersects State Highway 19 coming north from Martinsburg. Highways 54 and 19 join and run north to Laddonia. Leading off to the east is County Road BB taking the traveler toward Middletown, Montgomery County, Missouri.

The story of Scott's Corner begins not in Audrain County, or Missouri, or even the United States, but rather in merry old England. The tale originates in 1860 with the birth of James Scott, Jr., the youngest of four boys, born to James, Sr. and Jane Scott. William, 5, George, 3, and Thomas, 1, with the addition of baby James made up the family living near Bristol.

Big changes were in the offing for this group. By the time James was one year old the family was preparing for a journey, a trip to America. The trek began in Liverpool, England in 1861. Deep inside the City of Manchester,[2] a steamer, the family was headed for New York. The ship's manifest shows the location of their accommodations aboard. The family was placed in the bottom hold. This is not a good place to be aboard ship. They abide and the ship arrived on 11 Mar. 1861 in New York Harbor.[3] Within a month America was torn apart by the Civil War.

The Scotts spent the next few years farming in Illinois. It may have been a group known to each other that came to Macoupin County, Illinois from England. Two more boys were added to the family, John and Edward.

On 21 August 1867 James bought 75 acres of land from Andrew Allen, also of Macoupin County for $950.[4] He was soon to be a resident of Audrain County, Missouri. His land was in Section 26, Township 51 north, Range 7 west, on the Grand Prairie. His farm was located in the northwest quarter of the section and was in Linn Township near the Johns Branch Post Office.

Thomas Edwards had come to the United States in 1857 and had also settled in Macoupin County, Illinois. Two years later, his wife, Mary Bradford Edwards, and one of his sons, William, died. Three other children survived. They were; George H., Louisa, and Thomas. In 1863 Thomas Sr. married a widow, Margaret Harrison
102

Whippell in St. Louis. She had a daughter by her first marriage, Jessie Whippell.[5]

After farming in Illinois for a number of years, he, like James Scott, came to Audrain County. In the fall of 1872 he purchased 120 acres of land in the southwest quarter of Section 26 from William L. French.[6] By then James Scott Sr. owned the other 40 acres in the southwest quarter.

James Scott died in 1875 and was buried in the West Cuivre Cemetery.[7] His wife, Jane, continued living on the original farm.

The next year on December 20, 1876, James' oldest son, William B., married Melissa Pierce.[8]

On the 13th of December 1882, Jessie [Whippel] Edwards became the wife of James H. Scott, Jr.[9]

George H. Edwards also married in December 1882, on the 22nd.[10] He wed Mary A. McNama, whose family lived in the same community, east of Johns Branch. The McNama family also came from Illinois. George and Mary's first child, Edna, was brought into the world by Dr. Van Deventer of Wellsville on 9 November 1883.[11] Their son, Edward, was born in 1887.

John R. Scott and Thomas Scott, brothers of William and James, married on the same day in 1889, the 13th of August. John married Sarah G. Dickey at the bride's house[12] and Thomas married Mary B. Bradford at his brother James' house.[13]

After his marriage, George farmed the second of Thomas Edwards' two farms. It was one hundred sixty acres, made up of two eighty acre plots across the road from each other, one-half mile north of the future Scott's Corner.

James and Jessie's beginning farm was one mile south of the Corner. He owned 80 acres east of the road. Jessie's stepfather, Thomas Edwards, had purchased the north half of the southwest quarter in section 36. James farmed the south one-half.

In 1887 Jane Scott and Thomas Edwards, along with several Audrain Countians returned to Europe for a visit. Two others who accompanied them were Christian Nohrnberg and Julius Krieger.[14] While Jane and Thomas were going to England, Christian and Julius were traveling to Germany. Christian farmed two miles west of Jane's farm. Julius was a storekeeper in Martinsburg.

Melissa Scott died in May 1887 and was buried at Laddonia. William B. married Mary E. Woodward in November of that year.[15]

In 1888 Thomas Edwards died on the 24th of February. He was buried on the 25th in Laddonia.[16] Margaret eventually moved back to St. Louis. She died there on December 20, 1896 and was buried in Laddonia the next day.[17]

George took over the original 120 acre farm of his father. His farm was then 280 acres. James and Jessie received the north half of section 36.

John R. Scott's wife, Sarah, died in 1891 at age 22.[18] He later married Nettie M. Ridgway, who at 28 died in 1898.[19] John married a third time to Bessie Huffman.[20]

A sad situation arose in 1892 or sooner in the George H. Edwards family. It seems that Mary McNama Edwards, George's wife became ill. It was tuberculosis or consumption. A decision was made to move to California for her health. On the 26th of August in 1893 Mary died in Los Angeles. She was survived by her husband and two children in Los Angeles. In Laddonia, she left her father, William McNama and two brothers. She also left two sisters of California and one sister of Illinois.[21]

On December 3, 1894, an event occurred which shocked the community and brought great sorrow to the Scott family. Jane Scott was living with one of her six sons, John R. Scott. At noon she had made preparations for his dinner.

When he came to the house, he found his mother had committed suicide by cutting her own throat with a razor in the sitting room. Her windpipe was severed and she died in a few minutes.

Her obituary stated, "Mrs. Scott had for a long time entertained the idea that she was going crazy and the thought must have temporarily unsettled her mind, and in a fit of despondency she took her own life."[22]

A family story says that Jane was suffering pain from some health issue. She was taking laudanum for this pain and that was the source of her mental condition. Laudanum is known as tincture of opium, and contains 10% powdered opium in an alcohol base. This story also avers that the deed was done before a full-length mirror in the sitting room. Normally, it was said, Jane was usually in a happy frame of mind and was a pleasant person to be around. Her body was laid to rest beside her husband in West Cuivre Cemetery. She was 63.[23]

Graves of James and Jane Scott, West Cuivre Cemetery

In 1894 Jim Scott added an 80 acre piece of land to his farm. This land was his first property on Scott's Corner. It was on the southwest part of the corner. One of his barns still exists there, all that is left of the Scott farmstead.

About 1894 George Edwards sold the original Thomas Edwards farm to Jim. It was 120 acres in the southwest quarter of Section 26. Jim also added 40 acres of his mother's farm for a total of 160 acres, the whole southwest quarter. In 1896 he added a 10 acre wood lot in Cuivre Township in Section 27 on the north bank of Cuivre River. In 1897 he purchased the 80 acres where Community R-VI School now stands in Section 25. It is on the northeast corner of Scott's Corner. In 1898 Jim obtained the block of land, 80 acres, on the northwest corner of Scott's Corner in Section 26. This became his home and farm headquarters. It is where the beautiful park with its big trees and picnic tables used to be before the highway department obliterated it in favor of a parking lot. This is the time and place where Scott's Corner became Scott's Corner.

George H. Edwards was a widower in California. He owned a newspaper route and continued in the news circulation business the rest of his life.[24] He married again. His second wife was Alma V. Edwards. His daughter, Edna, married George Gairing. His son, Edward, also worked in the newspaper business.[25]

Another family story emerged concerning a sad turn in Jim Scott's life. The tale is told that he ran for a county office in Audrain County. Just when this happened is not known. At this point the writer has been unable to find evidence of this try for office. Jim Scott, however, was a dyed in the wool Republican running in a Democratic county. The result was obvious, he lost. He did develop a penchant for strong drink at this time and this led to alcoholism. He seems to have been plagued with this problem for the remainder of his life.

Around the turn of the twentieth century, it was a popular idea to name one's farm. The 1898 Plat Book for Audrain shows many of the names farmers had chosen. To the east of Jim Scott's place was R. C. Darlington's Maple Grove Stock Farm. To the north was Jacob Freyer's Evergreen Stock Farm and west of him was W. P. Kennedy's Osage Stock Farm. East of Freyer's was Mrs. A. S. Hale's Hickory Valley Farm on Johns Branch. Henry Youngblood was east of her with Cedar Grove Stock Farm. Southeast of Jim's was Joseph Fennewald's Pine Lawn Stock Farm and west of him was Barney Fennewald's Prairieview Stock Farm. Jim Scott's choice reflected his wife's stepfather as previous owner. He called his farm, Edwards Stock Farm. On this farm west of his house and at the top of the hill was Edward's School.[26]

In 1900 Jim and Jessie had eight children, seven of whom were living. He was 39 and Jessie was 38.[27] Jim's brothers, William B. and George F. moved to Furnas County, Nebraska. Edward lived in San Benito, Texas.

By 1910 Jim had either swapped or sold his original farm of 160 acres, one mile south of Scott's Corner. He owned the two eighties that George Edwards had just north of Scott's Corner, that had been owned by Ben Kemna. He now had 320 acres in section 25 and 320 acres in section 26.

Financial troubles seemed to be looming on the horizon. He appears to have been borrowing money against his land from Northwestern Mutual Insurance Company. By 1913 they owned the 80 acres on the southwest corner of the Scott farm. A pencil written note in the 1913 Tax Assessment Book for Audrain County[28] shows that the 320 acres in section 25 was split with Northwest Mutual listed on the north ½ of it with the figure $940. The same was true for the north ½ of section 26 with the same figure $940. Also the western 160 acres (the old Thomas Edwards farm and the 40 acres owned by his father) were also penciled in to Northwest Mutual with the figure $1900.

By 1915, Northwest Mutual Insurance Company owned all of that land. Jim Scott still had his homeplace on the north side of the corner and the 80 to the east across the road.

The 1918 Audrain Atlas[29] shows plainly Jim Scott's fall from grace. Scott's Corner took the name and carried it into the future.

James H. Scott, Jr. married Mabel Mollring in Mexico on 15 June 1920.[30] Within a few years he also moved to Furnas County, Nebraska. By 1930 he was the Treasurer of the county. His youngest sister, Jessie, married Finley Johnson in Mexico on 22 December 1923.[31] They honeymooned in Nebraska.

Jessie Fremont Edwards Scott died at age 69 on Sunday, 22 February 1931[32] after a long illness. James Scott was to have a public sale on March 9, 1931, but heavy rains made the roads impassable. It was postponed until the 13th of March.[33]

On the 27th of October 1931, the Monitor told the story. "HIGHWAY LANDMARK IS DESTROYED BY FIRE TUESDAY NIGHT – One of the famous landmarks, marked on all State Road Maps as Scott's Corner, was totally destroyed by fire Tuesday night about ten o'clock. It was the old Jim Scott residence, a two story frame house, located on a triangular piece of ground, created by the intersecting of Highways 54 and 19."[34] The farm was owned by an insurance company and some renters were living there.

In the following years he divided his time between living with James, Jr. in Nebraska and his daughter, Jessie Johnson, in Audrain. He broke a hip in December of 1941 and died January 2, 1942.[35] He and Jessie are buried in the Laddonia Cemetery.

His obituary closed with the statement, "In politics he was one of East Audrain County's most prominent Republicans."[36]

Audrain County doesn't have a lock on the Scott's Corner name. There is a Scott's Corner, Minnesota. In Kings County, Nova Scotia, Canada, we find Scott's Corner. Scott's Corners appear or have appeared in Maine, New Jersey, and Ohio. In California, Scott's Corner was named for Thomas Scott, who had a store in the 1850s, supplying men headed for the gold fields. The Pound Ridge, New York, Volunteer Fire Department is in Scott's Corner.

The name has been used for markets, shopping centers, bars, hay and feed stores, golf courses, flower shops, and cemeteries. Even a Civil War battle was called the Battle of Scott's Corner, Virginia.

When we see how numerous the name, Scott's Corner, seems to be across the United States, we must also remember that the United Kingdom has made extensive use of the name in large numbers.

HIGHWAY HISTORY

When the writer first envisioned a story of Scott's Corner, he planned to highlight the Scott family and how Scott's Corner got its name. He then realized that this corner was a meeting of roads and that the story of the roads needed to be told. In researching the history of the highways, he discovered a fascinating tale of roads, road supporters, detractors, and local and state pitched battles over where roads would be located.

An Indian trail originating in the area of St. Charles and running northwest along the south side of Cuivre River cut across what is today Audrain County. This trail was called the Great Trail or by some, Nemacolin's Path. In later times the trail morphed into the St. Charles-Mexico Road. It is easily traced on the maps of Audrain County.

Incidentally this road angles past the West Cuivre Cemetery, where the elder Scotts lie in eternal rest.

This road had a St. Louis connection. "In 1837 the St. Louis and St. Charles Turnpike Company was incorporated. It was 1865 before the company got around to reporting that the entire road between St. Louis and the Missouri River opposite St. Charles had been constructed of rock. Thus, it came to be called the 'St. Charles Rock Road'."[37]

The St. Charles-Mexico Road held a position of importance in the early life of Audrain County. Goods moved up the road from St. Louis. People also followed this route into the county. West of St. Charles, the road was dirt and much of the time nearly impassable. As one traveler said, "If the mud does not get quite over your boot tops when you sit in the saddle, they call it a middling-good road."[38] Cuivre Township was populated early from this direction. The road held sway until the late 1850s, when the North Missouri Railroad began to make inroads into the flow of freight to Mexico.

The development of roads in Audrain County was slow even though they were needed to get products to market and especially to the railroad.

Newspaper editors and politicians were constantly calling for better roads. This continued through the latter half of the Nineteenth Century and into the Twentieth.

Good Roads Convention Poster – 1906

In 1911 a proposal was made in the legislature to build a road from St. Louis to Kansas City. The arguments went on for another ten years.

The Hawes Road Law created the State Highway Department. It shifted road responsibility from the county to the state. By 1917, sixty-one projects had been started under this law.

Counties set up county-seat highway commissions. One of the major projects for these commissions was to keep the county-seat dirt roads in shape. This was done by road dragging. It was paid for in 1921 from a road dragging fund at the rate of $15 per mile.

Dragging on other roads cost seventy cents a mile.[39] There were 134 miles of county-seat roads in Audrain County. The Eight Mile Road District contracted to drag the seven county-seat roads. The Eight Mile Road District appears to have been the road leading south from Mexico for eight miles.

John M. Malang, who developed exceptional roads in the Joplin Special Road District, became the first Superintendent of Missouri Highways. As superintendent at Joplin, he built the first concrete road on the state system from Webb City to the Kansas line. This was Federal Aid Project No. 2. This stretch of road became part of a highway called the Kickapoo Trace, the Wire Road, Route 66 and eventually Interstate 44.[40]

Malang authored the Morgan-McCullough State Road Law of 1919.[41] It was part of a state-wide movement to construct durable roads with state and federal aid under the new law. Malang promulgated a map of his road proposals in early 1921. One part of this proposed road would go east of Mexico to the Rush Hill corner. There the road would divide with one leg going straight to Laddonia and the other straight to Martinsburg. This quickly changed to going on east to Scott's Corner and then north and south to the above mentioned towns. The roads were designated as primary and secondary. Each county in the state were guaranteed at least two state roads.[42]

The impetus for these actions began to develop with the increasing use of automobiles. 1290 cars were licensed in Audrain County in 1917. By 1920 there were 2,657 registrations. Statewide there were 300,000 automobiles.[43]

Malang coined the phrase, "Lift Missouri Out of the Mud."[44] It spread like wildfire through the media. He wanted a two-cent state gasoline tax and vehicle registration to pay for building and maintaining roads.

The Federal Bureau of Public Roads was instituted within the Department of Agriculture. In Missouri a State Highway Board formed and they began road projects under Malang's leadership. In September of 1919 the Board approved eleven projects amounting to 58 miles of roads across Missouri.[45]

Newspaper articles in 1918 pointed out a trouble spot at the Chicago and Alton underpass at East Lake east of Mexico. It was called the East Lake Death Trap. Under the tracks a narrow one-lane passage off a sharp blind turn produced a dangerous situation. There was an intense desire to remedy this highway danger. Liberty Street did not come straight across the South Fork of Salt River at the time. There was a turn down to an old steel bridge.[46]

In February of 1921 the changes needed at the East Lake Death Trap still had not been started. The government originally had pledged to pay part of the cost. They then took an opposite position. It was felt the work should be started as soon as possible.

"In commemoration of Missouri's 100th year of statehood, the first bipartisan State Highway Commission was created by the 'Centennial Road Law' in a special legislative session. This law shifted the focus of Missouri highway building from the local to the state level. On Dec. 1, 1921, Governor Arthur M. Hyde appointed Theodore Gary, chairman of the Commission."[47]

Names were being given to the various routes suggested in Malang's map. Civic organizations were formed in the towns through which the routes would pass. In Missouri the Pershing Way began at the Iowa line and ran south through Paris, Mexico, and Fulton. The full scope of this route was that it was designed to run from Winnipeg, Canada to New Orleans, Louisiana. The idea of the Pershing Way was a product of the Chamber of Commerce at Cedar Falls, Iowa.

Herbert F. McDougal, who managed the push for the Pershing Way from Cedar Falls, Iowa, was in Mexico in September, 1921. He reported 4000 members of Pershing Way Clubs in 250 communities along the 2000 mile route.[48]

The North Cross State Highway was an east-west road planned to go from Hannibal through Mexico to Glasgow on the Missouri River. From there it would go west to Marshall and Kansas City. A spur would reach south from Hannibal to Louisiana. This road took on the name, The Golden Belt Route. On May 5th, 1921 a group of boosters for this road met in Mexico. They took their request before the State Highway Commission later in the month.[49]

The people of Glasgow and the surrounding area raised $400,000 as a carrot for the Commission to build a bridge there. They were in competition with a group from Booneville, who wanted a bridge built there for the Old Trails Route.[50]

The National Old Trails Road was to go from St. Louis to Kansas City. They planned to put granite markers every mile with the names of the soldier dead of county or town. By 1921 there was a push to pave this road as a memorial to the heroes of World War One.[51]

The Glacier Trail was another desired route to the west of Audrain County. It was in competition with the Pershing Way. It was touted by supporters in Columbia, Moberly, Macon, and Kirksville. The Commercial Clubs of Columbia and Kirksville led the way. This was to be the path to Glacier National Park.[52] The writer is reminded of a road in Montgomery County called Glacier Trail that in some way must be a vestige of this idea.

It is amazing that the popularity of the automobile grew so swiftly. When car builders like Ford brought down the cost, aver-

110

age people flocked to buy cars. With car owners increasing in number the clamor for good roads rose to a din.

Boosters found in towns along prospective routes raised the discourse to a fever pitch. People were willing to put money into the mix. The citizens of Glasgow offered $400,000 for their pet bridge, while the people of Booneville raised $300,000 for theirs. Similar generosity was found in most of the clubs and organizations backing their favorite highways.

With their new automobiles people traveled. Even without good roads they became tourists. The Grand Canyon, Yellowstone, and Glacier National Parks as well as many other tourist destinations were visited by people driving long distances on terrible roads in less than comfortable cars. The tourist dollar was added to the desires of the road booster. Good roads to your attraction meant more money coming to your town.[53]

In October, 1921, discussion arose within the Highway Department to take some of the North State Highway funds and use it to raise the Burlington tracks four miles east of Mexico. There was opposition to this idea, and nothing definite was done.[54] Years later the highway was raised over the tracks with an overpass. With the demise of this railroad the overpass was dismantled.

The Federal Bureau of Public Roads, U. S. Department of Agriculture, produced national policy for roads. This authority was passed to the states and their state highway commissions. They had the unenviable task of bringing order out of chaos, picking winners and declaring losers. There was a need to determine the major routes and get them marked. In November, 1921, the President signed the new Federal Highway Bill. Federal monies were being distributed for road construction. Missouri's share amounted to $2,448,128.[55]

Theodore Gary of Macon, Missouri was appointed chairman of the Highway Commission in 1922 as a result of the Centennial Road Law of 1921. As a public spirited citizen, he wanted the very best information possible on carrying out the road plan in Missouri. He hired one of the three leading highway engineers in the United States. He personally paid the $12,000 salary himself.[56] Imagine such a situation today!

Work began in February, 1922, on the improvement of East Liberty Street in Mexico.[57]

By June a rumor was circulating that Mexico was not on the primary roads report. Moberly was placed on the preferred system of roads. This caused great agitation in Audrain County.[58]

Contractors were waiting for grading and culvert contracts on the road east from Mexico to the Burlington Crossing. It was believed they would be let in September.

Work was reported to have started on the North State Highway at Moberly. Grading to make the road ready for gravelling was begun.[59]

Also in September, 1922, it was announced by B. H. Piepmeier, chief highway engineer, that the highway between Kansas City and St. Louis would be built of concrete. The road would be eighteen feet wide with a black line down the center to divide the traffic. In addition two-thirds of the secondary roads would be gravel.[60]

Piepmeier included that bids would open on September 28, 1922. It would be for 2.76 miles of grading and gravelling east out of Mexico. Twenty-one counties would be affected by bid letting.[61]

The Missouri State Highway Commission issued a statement at that time saying that the communities which gave free right-of-way would be given construction preference. They showed plans for numbering the road system. Oval metal signs were decided upon for marking the roads. They were arranging for the publication of maps to aid the tourist.[62]

By October, number designations were given to the state's roads. From the Iowa line, Highway 7, The Glacier Trail, ran south through Moberly, Columbia, and Jefferson City. The North Cross State Highway or Golden Belt Route was numbered 22. Highway 45 ran from Scott's Corner to Martinsburg and south.[63] From Moberly to St. Louis one would travel on No. 7, The Glacier Trail, to Clark, No. 22, The North Cross State Highway, to Scott's Corner. Then one would go south on No. 45 to Danville and east on No. 2, the National Old Trails Road, to St. Louis.

The Bureau of Public Roads had by November, 1922, approved plans for the building of the bridge at Glasgow on the Golden Belt Route.[64]

In December bids were let for State Project 126, Highway 22. This work was to be on the East Highway from Mexico to the Burlington Crossing, 3.351 miles.[65]

The year 1922 ended with a North Road Meeting at Carrollton on December 28th.
They announced that they would be emphasizing the importance of the North Cross State Highway. The major speech planned was "Difficulties that cities and communities must meet and overcome in the construction of the state highway system."[66] Turner Williams was Mexico's delegate.

The meeting decided to print two color folders with a map showing the route unmistakably. The entire route from Moberly to Quincy was marked with the letters, "M" and "Q."

One must be reminded that with all the organizations clamoring for good roads there were also people in opposition to the plans. The dirt roads group supported Rep. Botts of Audrain County, who

112

introduced a bill to check the state road plan.[67] Botts continued working against hard surface roads. He led the fight to investigate concrete roads built in St. Louis as being inferior. There have always been opposition groups. In 1905, for example, an organization formed in Mexico called the Audrain County Anti-Automobile Association. It found supporters across Audrain including Martinsburg.

S. P. Emmons headed up the road dragging plan in Audrain County for the County-Seat Highway Commission. In January 1923, he began asking farmers to drag their own roads for $15 a mile. He wanted to use up the state money because he believed Audrain County would not get anymore from the state.

The year 1923 saw a major increase in the marking of roads. Eight hundred miles of Missouri roads were slated for markers to guide tourists. It was hoped that by midyear all 16,082 markers would be in place. The markers were oval in shape and one foot across. They had Missouri State Highway printed around the outside edge and the number in the middle. They were colored with black letters on an orange background. This was thought to be the most visible scheme. The signs would be placed four feet high so that auto lights would strike them.[68]

Highway Route Marker

An idea that was becoming more popular in road building circles was the idea of airline routes. In other words, the shortest distance between two points as an airplane would fly. This idea was being put into practice in the building of Highway No. 2, the National Old Trails Route. The towns along the route were being bypassed in favor of a straighter, shorter route between St. Louis and Kansas City. Forty miles were cut off the road distance and this made the road shorter than the nearest railroad route. The highway department believed future generations would applaud its vision.[69] The bridge at Booneville was progressing rapidly. The No. 2 road would eventually be 256 ½ miles long and plans were to complete it by 1928. The No. 2 would pass 17 miles south of Mexico and would be connected to Mexico by a hard surfaced branch road. When completed it was expected that 2,000 vehicles a day would use the highway.

In May 1923, it was learned in Mexico that Highway Project No. 7 from Hannibal to Moberly would come through Mexico on the North State Highway No. 22. This was a change from the plan to bring the highway through Paris. The reason for the change would mean fewer miles would have to be constructed. The move to hold down costs seems to have been gaining strength.[70]

In Audrain County, the idea of giving free right-of-way to the State Highway Commission ran into trouble immediately. Farmers were refusing to donate the right-of-way. This refusal caused all projects in Audrain County to be postponed except the East Highway work.

Judge S. C. Groves warned road improvements would be lost by having to go through condemnation proceedings to obtain right-of-way.[71]

A gravel road in Cuivre Township was suggested by George Adams, a road supporter of that area. The road would run from Vandalia south for five miles, then west into Laddonia. Then hopefully it would go south to the state road at Scott's Corner. No man in the township would be more than six miles from the road.[72]

"TWELVE MILES ALL WEATHER ROAD LEAD TO MEXICO BY FALL." This is the headline that graced the Ledger in February 1924. They interviewed Guy Hall, State Highway Engineer for Audrain County. He explained the three projects that would begin in March. Since the Beaver Dam Bridge at the east end of Liberty Street had been approved for construction, gravelling would start from there to the Chicago and Alton underpass. The fight was still on with the C. and A. over the approach to the underpass and how it was to be funded. The strip from the C. and A. spillway to just west of the Burlington crossing would be graded and graveled. The third project would be from the Burlington crossing to the Rush Hill road. The Ledger believes that once the right-of-way was secured to Scott's Corner, that section will also be graded and graveled. It was thought that the result would be a "splendid gravel road," twelve miles long east of Mexico by fall. An 800 foot side-track would be built at the Burlington crossing on right-of-way provided by the Fields family. Once built 700 carloads of gravel would be brought in for the work.[73]

Kyle Watkins, grandson of Fred Watkins of Martinsburg, was a map maker of considerable ability. A small state highway map and the new 5-foot square state map were his work. This new map would show every railroad, town, creek, and all highways and their

114

stage of construction and many other details.[74]

The new maps were part of a campaign to get a law passed to increase license fees by 50 per cent. It would include a 2 cent gasoline tax. These increases were for highway maintenance and to finish the construction of 7,640 miles of state roads. It was desired to bring the changes to a vote of the people. To do this the Automobile Club of Missouri sponsored petitions to be signed by the voters. Enough signatures were obtained.

In addition to the underpass problem at the C. and A. Railroad, there also was a problem with right-of-way procurement. Condemnation suits had to be brought against John J. Hildebrand, Henry Winkler, J. E. Sterner, and an Illinois landowner to get the necessary right-of-way. Gravelling started at the Burlington crossing and moved toward Mexico. The road was closed so that there would be no traffic interference.[75]

On the 19th of June it was reported that the right-of-way had been legally granted for the East Highway. Alex Paris, J. W. Fuhrer, L. H. Fuhrer, W. H. Fuhrer, Chas. Farrah, Mark Collins, Edward H. Blase, J. H. Stumpf, Samuel Shalton, Fred Alexander, Lizzie A. Field, French Field, Hardin Field, Harrison Field, Roy Field, Addie Field, and Roy Dudley granted land for the highway. It was stated that gravel was arriving slowly.[76]

A week later it was reported that R. D. Clark had given a deed for a mile strip of right-of-way between the Burlington crossing and the Rush Hill road. It also mentioned that the name of E. M. Boyes had been omitted from the list of grantors from the week before. He was the first to turn over a deed to right-of-way and he also circulated the petition of the Automobile Club of Missouri. The report said that Mr. Boyes had done other things that helped to hurry up the road work.[77]

The problems on the East Highway project continued. With gravel arriving very slowly and machinery breaking down in the gravel pits at Bowling Green, Kirby Raines, who had the contract for graveling the first four miles, loaded up his equipment and moved to another job. The road was under construction for over a year and the various delays were generally displeasing the public. Guy Hall did not know if or when Raines would return.[78]

Contractor Murphy was given the green light to build the new bridge on Liberty Street. He would also take down the steel bridge over the East Lake Spillway. He was to build the last four miles of the East Highway from the Rush Hill (Eureka School) corner to Scott's Corner.

Kirby Raines sent word that he would be back in ten days to finish the graveling of the last mile and a half of his contract.

The construction of the Young's Creek concrete bridge, 13

miles north of Mexico, was expected to start by the middle of September 1924.[79]

Theodore Gary announced that Amendment No. 5 had been adopted and would go into effect January 1, 1925. The increase in registration fees for autos and a two cents per gallon gas tax would bring in funds for highway maintenance and an interest fund for construction.[80] In 1923 Audrain had 3300 autos.

With the new hard surfaced roads there would come the necessity of protecting them from overweight truck traffic. New laws were expected to consider speeds and weights in an effort to save the roads from damage.

In late November J. K. Knoerle took over the state highway work in Audrain County. He stated that the Highway Department was going to try to complete the East Highway gravelling before freezing weather set in. He added that two groups of gravellers were going to work from east and west toward each other. Knoerle was also put in charge of the building of three major bridges in the county. He set up an office in Smith's Grocery in Mexico.[81]

Four projects were planned for Audrain County in 1925. Gravelling from Eureka School to Scott's Corner, a five-mile stretch of road near Vandalia, a three or four miles of gravel from the west county line, completing the bridges, and building the culverts on the Paris road was the work laid out by F. M. Settles. He worked out of the Hannibal office of the highway department. He was named an assistant to Mr. Knoerle. Mr. Settles said that the highway department intended to open Highway No. 15 clear through the state at the earliest possible time. Work on that route was being rushed. The Paris road would be graveled starting at the north county line and would work south to Mexico.[82]

Contracts for work on the Vandalia highway projects were to be let on 8 miles of road. The two four mile stretches will be from Vandalia west on State Highway No. 22, better known as the East Highway. The work included a bridge over Cuivre River. As of this writing a third Cuivre Bridge is being built.

First Cuivre Bridge, Photo 1954 Courtesy Missouri State Archives

The Ledger reported a rumor that a concrete road from Mexico to Fulton was possible. That road was thought to have been designated a primary road. This would have been the only primary road for Audrain County. A primary road could be made of gravel, concrete, or asphalt. The Audrain County Chamber of Commerce was working to back the road and get it built of concrete.[83] Route No. 15 would cross No. 2 at McCredie and continue on to Fulton. This airline route for No. 2 through McCredie was a shorter way than through Fulton by four miles. The Missouri State Highway Commission resolved to complete No. 15 south to Fulton and north to Mexico by 1926.[84]

Planning began in 1926 for a highway patrol to enforce the laws that would be needed.

In August of 1925 the East Liberty Street Bridge opened. E. A. Pickett, 402 West Maple, was the first person to drive over the new bridge. Motorists were told they could cross the new bridge on the way to the dedication of the boating pier at the country club without any detour.[85]

Mid-1926 saw the completion of the Scott-Fennewald Bridge over Mam's Slough, just west of Scott's Corner. While this bridge was being built, traffic was detoured one mile south of Scott's Corner, then one mile west and finally one mile north back to the roadway. Highway 22 was graveled between Farber and Vandalia.[86] When gravelling operations reached Scott's Corner to complete the route from Mexico to Scott's Corner, an important change was made in the road. Instead of 22 coming up to 19 as a ninety degree turn, the road was split and one curve was turned toward Martinsburg just missing Jim Scott's south barn. It was a sharper turn than the one which curved toward Laddonia. Jim Scott's farmstead now sat on a triangle of land isolated by roadways. Later in 1932 when the concrete was laid, construction followed the curves toward Martinsburg and Laddonia. Eventually the triangle was obtained by the Highway Department and the Scott's Corner Roadside Park was added as a rest stop for tourists and motorists.

Toward the end of 1926, the Federal government came out with the designations of Federal Highways. No. 7 became Highway 63. No. 2 was renumbered Highway 40. Highway 54 was laid out from Louisiana through Vandalia, Farber, Laddonia, Scott's Corner, Mexico, and went south from there to Highway 40 at McCredie. State Road 15 led only north from Mexico to Paris and 22 ran west from Mexico to the county line. The only hard surfaced roads were the road called the East Highway to Scott's Corner and eight miles south of Mexico. They were now both part of Federal Highway 54.

This changed in November when the road to Martinsburg was

finally graveled. The wet summer had slowed the work, but by Election Day the people of Martinsburg would always remember it as the day Highway 45 was completed to the east limits of town.[87]

1926 saw the resignations of two hardworking builders of the Missouri Highway System. Theodore Gary, chairman of the State Highway Commission, and B. H. Piepmeier, chief engineer, went to work together in the private sector. The chairman was replaced by Charles Buffum, president of LaCrosse Lumber Company in Louisiana. Buffum took up the reins on November 25, 1926.

Finally in June, 1928 the last section of Highway 54 was graveled. That part of the road ran from Scott's Corner to Laddonia. 54 now was a hard road with gravel and some concrete from Louisiana to Highway 40.[88]

Another $75 million road bond was passed with an amendment to the constitution. Primary and Secondary roads would continue to be built and maintained in Missouri. A portion of this money was to be spent on a "new idea," farm-to-market roads or feeder roads to the main highways. Farmers could then begin to think of selling their cattle and hogs directly in St. Louis by truck, rather than getting them to the local railroad.

Contracts were let in 1930 for the first two farm-to-market projects in the county, Rush Hill and Benton City. The bid for the Rush Hill gravel road was $16,891, while Benton City's route was bid at $13,049.[89]

By 1930 the highway connection between Mexico and Kingdom City was being concreted. Paving distances were reported by so many feet per day. By May they were averaging 586 feet per day. The concrete road to Kingdom City was finished at the end of May and in the same week the gravelling to Centralia was finished.[90]

It was announced that the highway east from Mexico to Scott's Corner would be paved. By past experience people realized that when an announcement was made it would be awhile before work began. Right-of-way had to be secured (in this case again), the engineers had to prepare the plans, bids had to be announced and let, preparations of the bed and grading, all had to be completed before the first foot of concrete was laid.

The Depression was in full swing. This had also slowed road construction. In February of 1932 the highway department began some work. It was decided to move the gravel from 54 and use it to resurface 45. Married men would be hired to work for three days and then they would be replaced by another group for three days and so on. The gravel was scraped up and loaded on trucks by hand.[91]

The plan called for 17 miles of concrete road from Mexico to

118

Laddonia in its final form. The road would be twenty foot wide, an improvement over the earlier 9, 10, or 18 foot slabs. Highway 45 would be renumbered Highway 19.

The pouring of concrete began in June 1932 at Edward's School, just west of Scott's Corner at the top of the hill. They worked west with bigger concrete mixers and set new records in the amount of pavement put down. On one day they put down 1864 feet of slab. They planned to work to the Burlington crossing and then move to Mexico and pave east.[92]

The next section poured was from Scott's Corner to Laddonia. It was finished by September.[93] The pouring continued on to Farber.

The pavement or "slab" as it was called, was poured with a six inch, 45 degree sloping lip or edge. This edge held water on the pavement in places that had to be drained away. At irregular intervals, depending on terrain, concrete spillways were placed channeling the water from the pavement into the ditches.

This lip had a plus side and a negative side. It did a good job of draining the water on the slab to the spillways and off the roadway. The writer can only guess, however, at how many accidents must have occurred when drivers ran up on the lip and lost control resulting in a crash. The spillways were also a danger. It was not unusual for a driver to pull off the road for some minor emergency, like a flat, and hit a spillway, which precipitated a major crash. In the spillway picture below the roadbank has been damaged by a flood. It is easy to see the lip of the road on the right, where the spillway joins the highway.

Concrete Drainage Spillway   Courtesy Missouri State Archives

Even with its drawbacks, the hard surface slab was a huge leap forward in the technology of improving roads.

The shoulders of the new paved highways also had to be finished. They were worked and seeded with grass. Rye seed was mixed in to shade the grass and give it a chance to grow. Straw was then spread over the seeding. Leo Hoer had the contract for seeding the shoulder of Highway 54 from Mexico to Laddonia. By October of 1932 the Highway Department had accepted the first five miles of seeding.[94]

Although right-of-way was being sought for Highway 19 in 1937, it was not until 1939 that the pavement was poured from Scott's Corner through Martinsburg to the county line. In 1941, two large reflector signs were installed at Scott's Corner by the Mexico Civics Club. They were large arrows pointing west with the name, Mexico, emblazoned across them. These Mexico signs were to aid motorists in making the correct turn at the junction of Highways 54 and 19. Many people were missing the turn and driving far out of their way, especially at night. One couple reported that they drove 50 miles before they discovered their mistake.[95]

Because of shortages of manpower, machinery and material, the efforts of road builders were hindered during World War II. Roads had been neglected during the war. After the war there was a push to better the supplementary roads of the state and maintenance and repair of existing roads was increased.

The twenty-year-old slab east of Mexico needed to be updated. It was deteriorating, too narrow, and the lip had to be eliminated. In 1954 a project in Audrain sought to remedy that problem. If you revisit the picture shown earlier of the Cuivre Bridge taken in 1954, you can see that the road has been resurfaced. Looking more closely you can see the seam in the pavement where the road was widened about 18 inches on both sides. The dangerous old spillways were also removed at that time. The picture below was taken south of Laddonia in 1954 and shows the old concrete slab at the Brown place. The new pavement was coming from the south to cover the 22-year-old slab.

Concrete Slab, s. of Laddonia,
Photo 1954 Courtesy Missouri State Archives

The writer hopes you found this look at highway history as interesting as he did. Creating our state's highway system was a very complex task. It was much more complex than the writer could convey with words.

In the memories of our highways there are millions of stories. Many of these stories are tragic with death, destruction, and agony. Some have more hopeful endings. To close this slice of history the writer would like to relate one of the dozens of stories he has witnessed, while living a lifetime next to the highway and also one told to him by his father.

There were two events, both dealing with diamond rings, both that occurred on Highway 54, two miles west of Scott's Corner. Although these happenings took place less than a quarter of a mile apart, they were separated by sixty-five years or more.

It was winter in the 1990's and a bitterly cold day. There was a high wind blowing snow across an icy roadway. Two women driving west lost traction and spun across the highway into the path of tractor trailer. The semi struck the automobile directly in the passenger side. It was a horrendous crash and both women were instantly killed. The driver of the car had been wearing a diamond ring of considerable size. A search of her person did not reveal the ring. Several searches were made and the ring was not located. It was a sad, macabre story.

In the following months the road ditch was searched three times with a metal detector. The ring was never found.

Now we go back to a time when Highway 54 was Highway 22. It was a gravel road. Preparations were being made for a new concrete "slab." This included removing old bridges and pouring concrete culverts. At this location the bridge had been removed. Since road safety was not a particularly important issue at the time, there was no signage indicating that the bridge had been removed.

A young married couple travelling the road at night ran off into the creek. The duo were thrown out of their touring car, but were not badly hurt. In the morning Mr. Hoer took his team of horses and pulled the car out of the creek. The two revealed that the wife had lost her diamond ring in the accident. The three spent some time searching for the ring with no luck.

A month later the couple came again to search the creek for the ring. This time the wife found her ring glittering in a riffle of water. It was a happy ending to a worrisome situation.

Two stories of a highway and diamond rings with very different endings. These are two of millions of stories our highways have witnessed.

The writer remembers a sampler his mother had sewn. It hung for years in the breakfast room of her home. It was read so many times that it was burned into his memory.

> Let me live in the house by the side of the road,
> Where the race of men go by.
> The men who are good, the men who are bad,
> As good and as bad as I.
> I would not sit in the scorner's seat
> Nor hurl the cynic's ban.
> Just let me live in the house by the side of the road
> And be a friend to man.[96]

Endnotes

[1]Martinsburg Monitor (Martinsburg, Audrain County, Missouri), 27 Oct 1927, Thursday, Vol. 8, No. 49, p. 1, col. 4. Hereinafter cited as Monitor.

[2]The City of Manchester had an iron hull with three masts and single smokestack. It had one screw that pushed the ship at 9 knots. It was built in 1851 and sailed as a steamer until 1871, when it was changed to a sailing ship. It wrecked in 1876.

[3]Ancestry.com. *New York Passenger Lists, 1851-1891* [database online]. Provo, Utah: MyFamily.com, Inc., 2003. Line 39, Microfilm Roll 208. National Archive Rolls: 95-580. National Archives, Washington, D. C.

[4]"Deed of Sale from Andrew Allen to James Scott," 21 Aug 1867 (filed 16 Dec 1867),   Audrain County Deed Records, Book Q, p. 435, Recorder's Office, Audrain County Courthouse, Mexico, Audrain County, Missouri.

[5]_____. History of Audrain County, Missouri (St. Louis: National Historical Co., 1884), p. 562. Hereinafter cited as History of Audrain.

Ancestry.com. *Missouri Marriage Records, 1805-2002* [database online]. Provo, UT, USA: Ancestry.com Operations, Inc., 2007.

[6]"Deed of Sale from W. L. French to Thos. Edwards," 18 Sep 1872, Audrain County Deed Records, Book I, p. 355, Recorder's Office, Audrain County Courthouse, Mexico, Audrain County, Missouri.

[7]"Grave of James Scott," West Cuivre Cemetery, Area F, Vol. 1, p. 156, Audrain Rd. 620, Audrain County, Missouri. Audrain County Area Genealogical Society, 305 W. Jackson St., Mexico, Missouri.

[8]"Marriage of William B. Scott and Melissa Pierce," 20 Dec 1876, Audrain County Marriages, Book B, p. 297, Recorder's Office, Audrain County Courthouse, Mexico, Audrain County, Mis-

souri. Hereinafter cited as Audrain Marriage Records.

[9]Monitor, "Marriage of James Scott, Jr. and Jessie [Whippell] Edwards," 13 Dec 1882, 26 Feb 1931, Vol. 12, No. 15, p. 1, col. 3.

[10]History of Audrain, p. 563.

[11]"Birth of Edna Edwards," 9 Nov 1883, Audrain County Births 1883-1885, Book 1, p. 27, Audrain County Area Genealogical Society, 305 W. Jackson St., Mexico, Missouri.

[12]Audrain Marriage Records, "Marriage of John R. Scott and Sarah Dickey," 13 Aug 1889, Book 2, p. 373.

[13]Audrain Marriage Records, "Marriage of Thomas Scott and Mary Bradford," 13 Aug 1889, Book 2, p. 373.

[14]Mexico Weekly Ledger (Mexico, Audrain County, Missouri),19 May 1887, Thursday, p. 3, col. 6. Hereinafter cited as Mexico Ledger.

[15]"Grave of Melissa Scott," Laddonia Cemetery, Lot 63, p. 10, Audrain County Area Genealogical Society, 305 W. Jackson St., Mexico, Missouri.

[16]The Intelligencer (Mexico, Audrain County, Missouri), 1 Mar 1888, Thursday, Vol. 16, No. 47, p. 6, col. 1. Hereinafter cited as The Intelligencer.

[17]Mexico Weekly Ledger (Mexico, Audrain County, Missouri), 24 Dec 1896, Thursday, Vol. 38, No. 39, p. 3, col. 9. Hereinafter cited as Mexico Ledger.

[18]"Grave of Sarah Scott," Wellsville Cemetery, p. 39, Row 4, No. 11, Montgomery County Historical Society, 112 West 2nd St., Montgomery City, Mo. Hereinafter cited as Wellsville Cemetery.

[19]Wellsville Cemetery, "Grave of Nettie Scott," p. 39, Row 4, No. 11.

[20]"Marriage License of John Scott and Bessie Huffman," 27 Sep 1904 (filed 29 Sep 1904), Audrain County Marriage Licenses, p. 206, Recorder's Office, Audrain County Courthouse, Mexico, Audrain County, Missouri.

[21]Mexico Ledger, 31 Aug 1893, Vol. 35, No. 22, p. 3, col. 8.

[22]The Intelligencer, 6 Dec 1894, Vol. 23, No. 36, p. 1, col. 6.

[23]"Grave of Jane Scott," West Cuivre Cemetery, Area F, Vol. 1, p. 156, Audrain Rd. 620, Audrain County, Missouri. Audrain County Area Genealogical Society, 305 W. Jackson St., Mexico, Missouri.

[24]1900 U. S. Census, District 57, Ward 1, Los Angeles, California; p. 6B, National Archives Roll: T623_90.

[25]1910 U. S. Census, District 231, Assembly District 70, Los Angeles, California; p. 6B, National Archives Roll: T624_80.

[26]_____. Plat Book of Audrain County, Missouri (Philadelphia: North West Publishing Co., 1898), p.14.

[27]1900 U. S. Census, District 5, Audrain County, Missouri; p. 3A, National Archives Roll: T623_837.

[28]Audrain County Tax Assessment Book 1913, pps. 47, 49, Audrain County Area Genealogical Society, 305 W. Jackson St., Mexico, Missouri.

[29]_____. Standard Atlas of Audrain County, Missouri (Chicago: Geo. A. Ogle & Co., 1918), p. 24.

[30]Audrain Marriage Records, "Marriage of James Scott, Jr. and Mabel Mollring," 15 Jun 1920, Book 10, p. 412.

[31]Monitor, 27 Dec 1923, Vol. 5, No. 6, p. 1, col. 3.

[32]Monitor, 26 Feb 1931, Vol. 12, No. 15, p. 1, col. 3.

[33]Monitor, 12 Mar 1931, Vol. 12, No. 17, p. 1, col. 6.

[34]Monitor, 29 Oct 1931, Vol. 13, No. 1, p. 1, col. 5.

[35]Monitor, 8 Jan 1942, Vol. 23, No. 11, p. 1, col. 3.

[36]Monitor, 8 Jan 1942.

[37]W. R. Nunn, Preparer. Roads & Their Builders (Missouri State Highway Commission), no copyright date, p. 21. Hereinafter cited as Roads & Their Builders.

[38]Roads & Their Builders, p. 21.

[39]Mexico Ledger, 17 Feb 1921, Vol. 62, No. 52, p. 1, col. 6.

[40]Roads & Their Builders, p. 65.

[41]modot.missouri.gov/about/Commission/CommissionGeneralinfo.htm *Missouri Highways and Transportation Commission – General Information*, p. 1, [data online]. Accessed 1/6/2011.

[42]Ibid., p. 1.

[43]Mexico Ledger, 17 Feb 1921.

[44]Mexico Ledger, 17 Feb 1921, Vol. 62, No. 52, p. 5, cols. 5,6.

[45]Mexico Ledger, 4 Sep 1919, Vol. 61, No. 28, p. 2, col. 2.

[46]Mexico Ledger, 1 Aug 1918, Vol. 60, No. 23, p. 3, col. 5.

[47]Roads & Their Builders, p. 65.

[48]Mexico Ledger, 15 Sep 1921, Vol. 63, No. 30, p. 3, cols. 1,2.

[49]Mexico Ledger, 5 May 1921, Vol. 63, No. 11, p. 1, col. 5.

[50]Mexico Ledger, 8 Jun 1922, Vol. 64, No. 16, p. 4, col. 4.

[51]Mexico Ledger, 14 Jul 1921, Vol. 63, No. 21, p. 4, col. 1.

[52]Mexico Ledger, 24 Feb 1921, Vol. 63, No. 1, p. 5, col. 3.

[53]Mexico Ledger, 15 Sep 1921.

[54]Mexico Ledger, 13 Oct 1921, Vol. 63, No. 34, p. 1, col. 6.

[55]Mexico Ledger, 17 Nov 1921, Vol. 63, No. 39, p. 2, col. 5.

[56]Mexico Ledger, 5 Jan 1922, Vol. 63, No. 46, p. 3, col. 2.

[57]Mexico Ledger, 23 Feb 1922, Vol. 64, No. 1, p. 2, col. 5.

[58]Mexico Ledger, 8 Jun 1922, Vol. 64, No. 16, p. 4, col. 4.

[59]Mexico Ledger, 7 Sep 1922, Vol. 64, No. 29, p. 7, col. 6. Mexico Ledger, 14 Sep 1922, Vol. 64, No. 30, p. 2, col. 4.

[60]Mexico Ledger, 14 Sep 1922, Vol. 64, No. 30, p. 3, col. 7.

[61]Mexico Ledger, 21 Sep 1922, Vol. 64, No. 31, p. 2, col. 6.

[62]Mexico Ledger, 28 Sep 1922, Vol. 64, No. 32, p. 2, col. 7.
[63]Mexico Ledger, 26 Oct 1922, Vol. 64, No. 36, p. 3, col. 2.
[64]Mexico Ledger, 2 Nov 1922, Vol. 64, No. 37, p. 2, col. 5.
[65]Mexico Ledger, 7 Dec 1922, Vol. 64, No. 42, p. 12, col. 5.
[66]Mexico Ledger, 21 Dec 1922, Vol. 64, No. 44, p. 7, col. 3.
[67]Mexico Ledger, 18 Jan 1923, Vol. 64, No. 48, p. 2, cols. 5,6.
[68]Mexico Ledger, 22 Feb 1923, Vol. 65, No. 1, p. 3, col. 5.
[69]Mexico Ledger, 24 May 1923, Vol. 65, No. 14, p. 3, col. 1.
[70]Mexico Ledger, 31 May 1923, Vol. 65, No. 15, p. 1, col. 1.
[71]Mexico Ledger, 5 Jul 1923, Vol. 65, No. 20, p. 1, col. 5.
[72]Mexico Ledger, 22 Nov 1923, Vol. 65, No. 40, p. 1, col. 7.
[73]Mexico Ledger, 21 Feb 1924, Vol. 66, No. 1, p. 3, cols. 1,2.
[74]Monitor, 5 Jun 1924, Vol. 5, No. 28, p. 1, col. 1.
[75]Mexico Ledger, 24 May 1924, Vol. 66, No. 15, p. 7, col. 4.
[76]Mexico Ledger, 19 Jun 1924, Vol. 66, No. 18, p. 7, cols. 5,6.
[77]Mexico Ledger, 26 Jun 1924, Vol. 66, No. 19, p. 1, col. 3.
[78]Mexico Ledger, 7 Aug 1924, Vol. 66, No. 25, p. 7, cols. 3,4.
[79]Mexico Ledger, 11 Sep 1924, Vol. 66, No. 30, p. 1. col. 7.
[80]Mexico Ledger, 13 Nov 1924, Vol. 66, No. 39, p. 7, col. 4.
[81]Mexico Ledger, 27 Nov 1924, Vol. 66, No. 41, p. 10, col. 5.
[82]Mexico Ledger, 15 Jan 1925, Vol. 66, No. 48, p. 1, cols. 6,7.
[83]Mexico Ledger, 19 Mar 1925, Vol. 67, No. 5, p. 2, cols. 4,5.
[84]Mexico Ledger, 25 Jun 1925, Vol. 67, No. 16, p. 1, col. 2.
[85]Mexico Ledger, 27 Aug 1925, Vol. 67, No. 28, p. 1, col. 2.
[86]Monitor, 13 May 1926, Vol. 7, No. 25, p. 1, col. 4.
[87]Monitor, 4 Nov 1926, Vol. 7, No. 50, p. 1, col. 6.
[88]Mexico Ledger, 28 Jun 1928, Vol. 70, No. 20, p. 1, col. 1.
[89]Monitor, 8 May 1930, Vol. 11, No. 26, p. 1, col. 5.
[90]Monitor, 5 Jun 1930, Vol. 11, No. 30, p. 1, col. 4.
[91]Monitor, 4 Feb 1932, Vol. 13, No. 15, p. 1, col. 4.
[92]Monitor, 30 Jun 1932, Vol. 13, No. 36, p. 1, col. 6.
[93]Mexico Ledger, 1 Sep 1932, Vol. 74, No. 69, p. 5, col. 3.
[94]Monitor, 6 Oct 1932, Vol. 13, No. 50, p. 1, col. 5.
[95]Monitor, 23 Oct 1941, Vol. 22, No. 52, p. 4, col. 4.
[96]Sam Walter Foss. "The House by the Side of the Road."
Dreams in Homespun. Boston: Lothrop, Lee & Shepard Co., 1897.
Pps. 11-12.

Crumbs

Martinsburg Monitor (Martinsburg, Audrain County, Missouri),
27 Feb 1930, Thursday, Vol. 11, No. 16, p. 1, col. 6.

TRUCK BAN IS ON
Heavy Loads are Being Kept Off Highway 19 and 54
Between Scott's Corner and Mexico.

On account of the weakened condition of Highway 19 between the Scott Corner and Mexico, all trucks are being turned back. Several came in here and unloaded their cargo to go on by [railroad] freight. All traffic is coming in from the east, as that section of the highway is in good condition. The heavy trucks have done much damage to the highways and it is a wise move to have the roads patrolled, as is now being done, but better judgment must be used on the matter.

The restriction is causing much inconvenience here. Louis Robinson who was moving the household goods of Wm. Shire to Mexico Tuesday was turned back at Scott's Corner. He had a light load, but the patrol would not let him go on. The Baer Motor Truck Company sent a truck from St. Louis to split a load held up and the patrol, it was said, would not let their empty truck use the highway. A few more days of dry weather and constant dragging will put the highway back in first class condition.

Mexico Weekly Ledger (Mexico, Audrain County, MO), 16 Nov 1876, Thursday, Vol. 18, No. 30, p. 8, col. 5.

TAX COLLECTOR'S NOTICE

Notice is hereby given, that the Collector of Audrain County will meet citizens of the various Townships at the following times and places; hereafter mentioned, for the purpose of collecting the Taxes for the year 1876. Viz:

Linn Township – Walker's School House, Monday, Tuesday and Wednesday, Oct. 23, 24 and 25.

Prairie Township – Keor or Botts School House, Thursday, Fri day, and Saturday, Oct. 26, 27 and 28.

Cuivre Township – Elzea's School House, Monday, Oct. 30; Crow's School House, Tuesday, Oct. 31; Vandalia, Wednesday, Nov. 1.

Loutre Township – Martinsburg, Thursday, Friday and Saturday, Nov. 2, 3 and 4.

The Bell Mystery

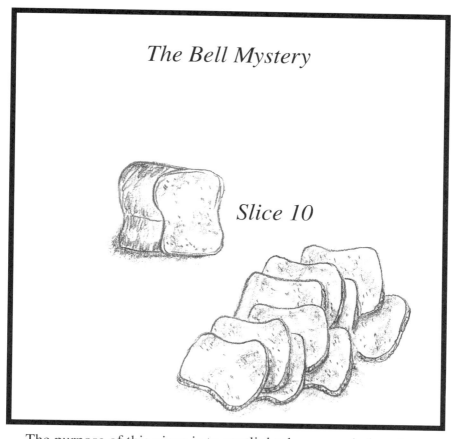

Slice 10

The purpose of this piece is to spotlight the research done by Albert Aulbur on the church bell at St. Joseph Catholic Church, Martinsburg, Missouri. In preparation for the hundredth anniversary of the church in 1976, he delved into the mystery of it's origin.

As a child, the nuns told the writer this story. The bell had once hung in the state capitol at Jefferson City. When the capitol was destroyed by fire, it was salvaged. Father Haar, Martinsburg's first resident priest, who was a native of Jefferson City, was able to obtain this bell. It was installed in the second church built at Martinsburg by him in 1886. As a child the writer was duly impressed by such an important bell with a fascinating history right here in the church at Martinsburg.

Alas, Albert began to see holes in the story. Studying the history of the state capitol building, he was startled by his discovery. The first state capitol in Jefferson City was built in the period 1823-1829 and was destroyed by fire in 1837. A new building was under construction at the time, and was completed in 1840.

The second capitol was destroyed by fire on February 5th, 1911, when a flash of lightning struck the dome. The present capitol was built in the period of 1912-1917. It stands on the same spot as its predecessor, high atop a bluff overlooking the Missouri River.

Albert next examined the bell high in its tower. He took pictures of it beneath its cover of guano deposited by the local birds. The bell was poured by B. R. Mayer & Co., St. Louis, in 1856. Cast into the bell were a picture of Jesus, another of Mary and Jesus, and a third that might be George Washington. They seemed an odd assortment of illustrations for a bell in the state capitol. The 1856 date was the clincher.

Photo of St. Joseph Bell, Striker shown lower left.

The wonderful story of the bell was simply not true. The Sisters of the Most Precious Blood would have been mortified.

Mr. Aulbur continued his search. When he contacted Rev. John W. Buchanan at St. Peter Church, 216 Broadway, Jefferson City, Missouri, he gained some additional valuable insights. St. Peter Church is southwest of and near to the Missouri State Capitol. This may have added impetus to the story.

The second St. Peter Church was built in 1858. It had a bell hung on a scaffold outside the church. Writers of the time said it, "looked like a gallows."[1] This church was torn down in 1882-1883 and a third church was built. It had four bells hung in the tune of

C sharp major. There was no need for the extra bell. Father Haar was assistant pastor there at the time, so he would have known about this bell.[2]

Father Haar was assigned to Martinsburg soon after and built a new church there. It seems reasonable that he laid claim to the extra bell and had it installed in his new church, St. Joseph Church.

"...it all adds up only one way, this is the bell that first hung on the outside scaffolding next to the second St. Peter Church in Jefferson City. Although it took a hundred years, I think we have the truth at last..."[3]

Father Joseph L. Haar continued as parish priest at Martinsburg until his death in 1917 at age 58. The writer's father was a pall-bearer for Father Haar. They took the train to Jefferson City and spent the night in a hotel. Father Haar was buried the next day at St. Peter's Cemetery on West Main Street. The cemetery, like the capitol, sits high above the Missouri River.

Albert Aulbur solved the mystery of the bell. It was reported at the 1976 Centennial Celebration of St. Joseph Church, Martinsburg, Missouri.

Endnotes

[1]Rev. John W. Buchanan to Albert Aulbur," 14 Aug 1976. Original letter in possession of the Aulbur family. Copy in possession of writer. Hereinafter cited as Buchanan Letter.

[2]Buchanan Letter

[3]"Albert Aulbur to Rev. John W. Buchanan," 26 Sep 1976, Copy of letter in possession of writer.

Crumbs

Mexico Weekly Ledger (Mexico, Audrain County, MO),
15 Jul 1880, Thursday, Vol. 22, No. 18, p. 2, col. 3.

MARTINSBURG

Pen Scratches by "Mother Mix"

Little do the good people of Martinsburg think there's a "chile amang them takin' notes." Nevertheless 'tis true, and we hope our scratches will be appreciated by the many readers of Bob White's paper. Martinsburg is slowly improving, John Coil's new hotel "looms up," and you can always find "rest for the weary" under his fatherly care. Charges, moderate. Our little city has been improved lately by the erection of a new depot, the boss one of its size on the road. Ed. is happy. He says anything is better than the old car. Our merchants are doing a good business. Reusch and Chetler, our new dry goods merchants, are building up a good trade. Tom Lowder, our blind grocer, is doing a thriving business. We understand that Hay Dillard of Shamrock, Callaway county, will open a hardware store in Smith's building about Sept. 1st. Come along, Mr. D., we need a good hardware merchant. After business comes pleasure, so a good many of the girls and boys took in the picnic at Wellsville on the 3rd inst. Miss Zoe Dillard of Mexico, is visiting Miss Mattie Marlow here. A large crowd from here attended Cuivre Church last Sunday. Bro. Marlow preached here last Sunday.

Laddonia Herald (Laddonia, Audrain County, MO),
7 Jan 1925, Wednesday, Vol. 41, No. 41, p. 1, col. 6.
Mrs. Teague Possesses Old Relic
Mrs. C. A. Teague handed us a paper Monday which will be interesting reading for our many readers, and we can hear them moan for the good old days gone by. It is a tax receipt of her fathers and it is written out in full, nothing printed about it, and it reads like this:

"Received of J. C. Thomas, two dollars and five cents in full of State and County tax for the year 1856 on 160 acre land, N. E. 13; 52; 7; Sept. 9, 1857. Franklin Cave, Clerk. By M. G. Duncan, D. C."

This is one of the many old relics that Mrs. Teague prizes highly.

Laddonia Herald (Laddonia, Audrain County, MO),
7 Jan 1925, Wednesday, Vol. 41, No. 41, p. 1, col. 5.
First Alumni Banquet Of L. H. S.
Thursday night for the first time in the history of the Laddonia High School, graduates of that institution met and honored their Alma Mater as [an] organized group.

Lewis Fox was chosen as President. Fred Hammett, Secretary and Treasurer of the organization.

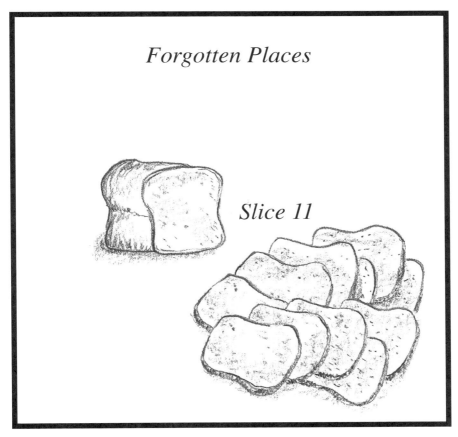

Forgotten Places

Slice 11

Have you ever heard of Barneyville over in Cuivre Township? Not many people have! It is one of Audrain County's forgotten places. These spots had an importance in their time, but history has overwhelmed them and they are little remembered. The writer has chosen twelve such locations. These dozen stories are brief, because little information has survived concerning them.

Much of the information about the places found here was taken from a master's thesis that was written by Esther Leech at the University of Missouri in 1933. She did a study titled, <u>Place-Names of Six East Central Counties of Missouri.</u> For each place she did historical research and then interviewed local people, who knew about the place and name.

Although the writer does not always totally agree with her analysis, she did do a monumental piece of work. He admires her labors and salutes her thesis.

Barneyville

Timothy Barney was a Pennsylvanian by birth. He came out to Missouri in 1835. Before he came here he was married to another Pennsylvanian, Catherine Sox. They settled on Cuivre and started a farm. For fifty years he provided his frontier hospitality to neighbor and traveler alike. One of his children was William N. Barney, who was born in 1842. In 1862, William joined the Enrolled Missouri Militia, a Union force, and served until the end of the war. William farmed beside his father until 1868, when he married a neighbor's daughter, Mary Frisby, daughter of James Frisby, who came from Illinois. Of their six children, three died as infants, one died at the age of twenty, and two girls lived to adulthood.[1]

Esther Leech states that Timothy Barney laid out the town named for him. She gave Nesbit Livingston and E. A. Shannon as her sources of information. Livingston was a Audrain probate judge at one time and Shannon was manager of an abstract company.[2]

The writer humbly differs with the particular statement that Timothy laid out the town. He believes the town was laid out in 1876 by William N. Barney. Timothy Barney would have been very old by this time and not long after moved to Texas to live with a daughter. The land where the town was platted was owned by William Barney. The town appears in the 1877 Atlas of Audrain County.[3] The Barneyville Post Office was opened in 1876 and closed in 1877. Nothing seems to have developed at Barneyville.

Barneyville was located in the southwest ¼ of the northwest ¼ of Section 29, Township 51 north, Range 5 west. It was situated on present-day Highway W. W leaves Highway B and heads north to Vandalia, crossing the Cuivre River. Barneyville lay on the east side of the road north of Cuivre.

Plat of Barneyville   1877 Atlas of Audrain County

Hickory Creek

The hunt for Hickory Creek in Cuivre Township was an interesting adventure, though the results are uncertain.

One source put the village south of Cuivre Creek on what had once been the St. Charles-Mexico Road. A nearby cemetery seemed to give credence to the story. The cemetery today is called the Fike, Field Cemetery. This is simply because those names have been found in it. Relatives of those named have searched through the brush and briars hunting for their ancestors. The true name of the cemetery apparently no longer exists. Could it have been Hickory Creek Cemetery?

This belief was altered, however, by a study of old maps, namely an 1855 and an 1869 Missouri map, showing the location to be north of Cuivre Creek. Both maps present Hickory Creek to be east of where Hickory Creek, a branch of Cuivre, enters Cuivre on the north bank.

Leech says the settlement was established at least by 1853 and had died out by 1876. This matches the opening and closing of a post office there in those years.

The surprise in this research was that the location east of Hickory Branch could be the same location as Barneyville. If Barneyville was platted in 1876, it seems reasonable to assume that Barneyville may have been an attempted resurrection of Hickory Creek. An on site inspection of this area, keeping the maps in mind, leads one to the same conclusion. This is an interesting supposition. Further study may yield some additional results.

These areas are grazing pastures for cattle today. There seems to be no vestige of Barneyville or Hickory Creek remaining today.

Johns Branch Post Office

Johns Branch is probably remembered today because a branch of Cuivre River begins just east of Scott's Corner and flows north to the river. It is named Johns Branch for an early settler by the name of Johns, who lived near Rush Hill. Many times an apostrophe is put between the n and s. This is incorrect as the man's name was Johns. O. M. Montague, a local Cuivre Township farmer, gave the information to Leech.[4]

The post office is not so well remembered. It was located two miles north of Scott's Corner on the east side of the road (Highways 54 and 19) in east Linn Township. It became a post office in 1855 and continued until 1878. In the beginning the post office was in the house of John Torreyson, who had settled at that place. Two of his brothers owned land on the east side of the present-day highway to the south of John. In 1877 it is shown in the Audrain Atlas as John's Store with the apostrophe.[5] It was at this location in 1863 that Margaret Torreyson, pioneer school teacher, was born.

Shy Post

Shy Post was a post office that was established on June 15, 1849 and located on Loutre Creek. It was called Shy Post for a Mr. Shy, who ran it. It was also called Loutre Post Office later. The post office even later was moved to the town of Martinsburg.

It seems impossible to give an exact location for Shy Post. No Mr. Shy has been located in the time period.

The name appears on an 1855 map of Missouri. It is shown on Loutre Creek. Only two other towns are shown in Audrain County at that time, Mexico and Hickory Creek.

Lake La Kota

This is a well-known place, but names change. Lake La Kota was a name given to the Chicago and Alton Railroad Lake or East Lake at Mexico. It was named when a countryclub and resort were built on it in 1920. The manager of the club was E. M. Lawder. The name was a result of combining two names, Lawder and Kota. Lawder provided the La and Kota, his wife's Christian name, was added, hence La Kota.

A boat dock on the lake was added in 1925. The club is still in operation today, but the name, La Kota, had faded into history. A lake just to the east of this one is called the Burlington Lake. The C. & A. RR and the Chicago, Burlington, and Quincy Railroad shared this stretch of track coming into Mexico. The two roads joined a little further east at a place called Francis Station. This is where the C. & A. RR from the northeast and the C. B. & Q. RR from the southeast met. Both railroads are now defunct. The southeast rails are gone completely. The northeast route is now a part of the Gateway Western system.

Francis Station

Francis Station stood just east of Mexico in Salt River Township. There was a coal tipple and a roundhouse there, the remains of the roundhouse are said to be visible today. It is unknown whether this is true. At one time, Leech reports that it was called Felton for Samuel Morse Felton, president of the C. & A. RR. Because it was often confused with Fulton in Callaway County, the name was changed. It became Francis for David R. Francis (1840-1927), Missouri's governor from 1889-1893. He was later prominent in national politics.[6]

E. M. Lawder of countryclub fame provided Leech with the information along with lawyer, Ed C. Kennan.

Haig

The railroads have provided several forgotten places. Haig is another of the railroad stations that are long gone. It lay on the C. B. & Q. RR, between Benton City and Highway 54. The blacktop still goes over the hump of the old rail bed there. The C. B. & Q. RR was built in 1904. Haig became a place with livestock pens, where farmers could bring their livestock, cattle and hogs, to be loaded on the train. It provided a route to the market in St. Louis. The shorter the distance the farmers had to drive their animals was a plus for them. These small stations, close-by, gave the feeders the incentive to make use of them. When roads were improved later, livestock was trucked directly to market and these stations went into decline. Eventually they were abandoned. In this case the railroad itself was finally closed. Grafton Station was one of these loading points near present Rush Hill. In its case, when Rush Hill was established and increased in importance, Grafton disappeared.

Littleby Station

Littleby Station was located about a mile west of Littleby Creek on the C. & A. Rail line. It lay between Rush Hill and Francis Station, possibly on the present day Fairchild farm. Like the other small stations, it too, had pens for livestock.

One other reason for a memory of it today is that in 1916 a C. & A. train went in the ditch there and crashed. There were many injuries, but unusual for such a wreck, there were no deaths. J. H. Fairchild was on the train and received minor injuries.[7]

Mount Carmel

The Mount Carmel neighborhood in Cuivre Township was the earliest settled part of the county. The area was pioneered by Pennsylvania Germans, Frenchmen, and Belgians. Mount Carmel was a centrally located trading point. Later in 1881 it gained a post office. This post office lasted until 1931 before it closed. The last postmaster was Gregory Douchant. He was born in Belgium and came with his father, Philibert Douchant, to Audrain County.

The name Mount Carmel is a Bible name. It is a mountain where Elijah overcame the priests of Baal. During Civil War times most of the county favored the south. Audrain provided some three hundred and fifty soldiers for the Union armies. About one half of Cuivre Township, especially the parts settled by Germans and Frenchmen around Mount Carmel Church, were pro-Union and eight out of ten joined the Union Army.[8]

Jefftown

This is another location that is hidden in plain sight. It is a place you know with a different name.

In this case the writer found an error in Leech's thesis concerning Jefftown. He can now tell you about Jefftown and give you the true story of its reason for being.

The town was originally named for Jefferson F. Jones of Callaway County. He was a flamboyant character in Callaway history. The idea of the Kingdom of Callaway comes from an incident in the Civil War in which he was involved.

Leech says he was instrumental in building the railroad through this town in northwest Loutre Township, east of Mexico. This road was the North Missouri built in 1857. Jones had nothing to do with that railroad. His plan came after the Civil War. It was to have the C. & A. Railroad build a line from Hannibal to Jefferson City. It would cross the North Missouri RR at Jefftown. The backers of Jones' idea bought up the land around Jefftown in readiness.[9] The railroad never materialized, going instead to Mexico.

In June of 1881 the town was named Benton City for Thomas Hart Benton (1782-1859), a senator from Missouri for thirty years.

Mam's Slough

A branch of Cuivre Creek called Mam's Slough rises in Loutre and Linn Townships. In Leech's thesis she recounts a story told to her by William Vivion. He must have been drinking dandelion wine on the day he spoke to Esther, as the tale he related seems to be such a reach as to be implausible. He said that a woman killed an animal on the creek bank. Since "maam slew," the creek was given the name Mam's Slough.[10]

As a boy the writer was told a more believable scenario by an old uncle. First, it must be remembered what a slough is or was. When the area was in primeval prairie, there were few places where the flow of water had cut down into the ground and created a creek. Much of that came after agriculture had destroyed the dense grass growth. Of course, large creeks and rivers had eroded to that extent. Instead there were swales, undulating dips in the landscape. These dips were marshy because the water was retarded in its path and moved very slowly through the grass. These swales or sloughs were wet even in the driest of times.

Understanding the slough, we next look at the Mam part of the name. As mentioned elsewhere in this work, a schoolmarm was born near (less than half a mile) from this slough. This was Margaret Torreyson, a well-known and popular pioneer teacher. Could the slough have been named for her or some other early teacher?

136

The morphing of marm into mam would not be unusual as spelling in pioneer times was very fluid. The writer believes that it is much more possible than transforming "slew" into "slough."

History keeps getting covered up and hidden. Now when you drive west from Scott's Corner toward Mexico, the first watercourse you cross is no longer called Mam's Slough as it was in the past. The highway department has now modernized the name with a sign, Mams Creek. The name is truthful, perhaps, but certainly less than historically endearing.

May William M. Vivion, born 1856 in Winchester, Kentucky, dying 1942 in Audrain, rest in peace.[11]

Endnotes

[1]_____. History of Audrain County, Missouri (St. Louis: National Historical Company, 1884), pps. 126, 127. Hereinafter cited as History of Audrain.

[2]Esther Gladys Leech. Place-Names of Six East Central Counties of Missouri (Master of Arts Thesis, University of Missouri, 1933), p. 16. Hereinafter cited as Place-Names.

[3]_____. Historical Atlas of Audrain County, Missouri (Philadelphia: Edwards Brothers of Missouri, 1877), p. 6. Hereinafter cited as 1877 Atlas of Audrain.

[4]Place-Names, p. 84.

[5]1877 Atlas of Audrain, p. 19.

[6]Place-Names, p. 63.

[7]Mexico Weekly Ledger (Mexico, Audrain County, Missouri), 8 June 1916, Thursday, p. 1, col. 2.

[8]Place-Names, p. 110.

[9]History of Audrain, p. 358.

[10]Mexico Ledger (Mexico, Audrain County, Missouri), 31 Dec 1994, Saturday, p. 2, cols. 4,5,6.

[11]Place-Names, p. 102.

[12]"Death Certificate for William M. Vivion," 21 Apr 1942 (filed 23 Apr 1942), File No. 13681, The Division of Health of Missouri, Jefferson City, Missouri 65101.

Crumbs

Mexico Intelligencer (Mexico, Audrain County, Missouri), 8 Dec 1892, Thursday, Vol 21, No. 36, p. 1, col. 4.

AFTER THIRTY YEARS

W. T. Toalson of Martinsburg, who suffered a surgical operation on one of his legs at the Baptist Sanitarium in St. Louis recently, was progressing nicely until a few days ago when erysipelas set in and he is now quite poorly. Mr. Toalson was wounded at the battle of Moore's Mill, in Callaway county in the early sixties, a bullet passing entirely through his leg and chipping off a small piece of bone. The wound healed rapidly and it was thought permanently, but after thirty years it began to trouble him and within the last year he has suffered much. The surgical operation was a successful one, particles of decayed bone being removed. Mr. Toalson was removed from St. Louis to his home in Martinsburg a few days before the election and was able to vote on the 8th.

The Martinsburg Enterprise (Martinsburg, Audrain County, MO), 15 Jan 1903, Thursday, Vol. 2, No. 51, p. 3, cols. 3, 4.

(Taken from the Vandalia Mail and Express).

The DeTienne Family

This was a large family that came direct from France and settled near Mt. Carmel, south of this city. Their ancestors were born in Warve, Belgium, a city of 17,000 inhabitants.

(Condensed: The trip from France to New Orleans took 68 days. Cholera claimed 75 lives during the passage and lasted till arrival. They came up the Mississippi River. At Cairo they passed 12 boatloads of immigrants stuck on a sand bar. They grounded too, but in a couple days they got loose and left the other boats stuck behind. Antoine and his nephew, Desire, worked in St. Louis that winter. The next spring they rented land, but drought destroyed the crop. The next year they had a good crop which they sold in the field and moved to this county (Audrain). It was in the Fall of 1855 when they settled at Mt. Carmel.

Antoine married a widow, Mrs. Marie Anna House. They adopted a neice, Miss Josephine, who married Henry Schultze, of near Farber. Desire DeTienne married Miss Leonnie Brabat. Six sons and a daughter were born to them.)

138

Patricide in Farber

Slice 12

As a juror, how would you have responded to parricide, the killing of a parent, or patricide, the killing of a father?

It was August 8, 1896 and Alexander January and his wife, Elizabeth, had returned to their farm home, a mile and a quarter north of Farber, Missouri. They had been to a picnic in Ralls County and had returned home late.

In the darkness of the barn, nineteen year old Willie, one of Alexander's thirteen children, waited with a double barrel shotgun. The barrels were loaded, the caps were on, and the hammers were half-cocked.[1]

Willie and several of his brothers had been having altercations with their father for over a year. On this Saturday night Willie planned to take action. As his father neared the barn, he came up behind Alexander and fired twice with the shotgun.

His mother, in the kitchen, heard the shots and also heard her husband call, "Oh, Will." She thought he had called William to help him with some chore.

The loads from the shotgun had hit Alexander in the left shoulder and and the left thigh. The latter blast penetrated into the stomach. His father, however, was not killed by the discharges. Willie then picked up a board and hit his father several times about the head and neck. These blows fractured and dislocated his jaw, cut and bruised his neck, and broke many smaller bones in the face. A five inch long wound was opened along the side of the head. This attack with the board ended Alexander's life. Willie hid the shotgun in the woodpile.[2]

Elizabeth, Willie's mother, went out to the well and saw Willie near his father. He called her over and she soon realized that Alexander was on the ground dead. She asked William who had hurt him.

He replied, "I did it to save my life and yours and the childrens."[3] He then told his mother he would go and tell the neighbors.

J. H. Franklin was asleep in bed when Willie arrived. It took time for Franklin to answer the door. Bert Sturgis and his brother had heard the shots. They were near Franklins,' and Willie told them his father had been murdered. When Franklin came, they all went to view the body. Franklin went to Farber to get the Constable. William said that his father had been killed by some unknown person, who had ridden off on horseback.

Coroner N. R. Rodes came to the scene Sunday morning. A jury was selected. It was composed of the following persons: Jenkins, Athey, Kendall, Alexander, Beshears, and Crow.

At the same time, Willie made a full confession to Constable M. N. Melson and Judge Alexander. He explained in detail how he carried out the murder. Willie was arrested and taken away to Mexico by Sheriff Stephens. An inquest proceeded.

Bert Sturgis testified to what he heard and saw. Dr. William May of Farber, as a witness, described the wounds he found on Alexander January's body. He felt the beating, not the shooting, was the cause of death.

Elizabeth came before the inquest and said that she had told Willie after the murder, "that he oughtn't to have done it." She stated that Willie had declared, "why mother, you know this morning that pa said he was going to kill us all and burn us up in the house after we were dead."[4]

She continued, saying that on the morning of the murder, the children had told her that their pa had a fuss with Willie and his brother, Robert.

Later pa went into the house and took his shotgun out with him. Elizabeth said she had been mistreated and abused by her husband on Friday night. He had thrown a case knife at her as well as some

140

potatoes and a bucket of water. She confided that Mr. January had slept with two pistols near him. He had told her that the bullets were molded for his own family. She related that a few days before, he had nearly killed one of the little children with a hoe. She yelled at him not to kill the child and he replied, "he would just as soon do it as not and he would cut Elizabeth's head off, too."[5]

The last witness was William Dye. He said he saw Willie about four o'clock Saturday, leaving Farber with a shotgun. Will had said that he had borrowed the gun from Mr. Clark.

William January was put on the stand, but he made no statement. The jury called for Willie to be bound over for the murder of his father.

On 12 August 1896 a preliminary hearing was held before the J. P.s Winscott and Jenkins in Farber. W. W. Botts of Vandalia was William's attorney. The Prosecuting Attorney was John D. Orear of Mexico. Willie again made no statement.[6]

Alexander January was born in Illinois in 1836. By 1850 his mother, Susanna, was a widow. Her son, Jonathan, was 18 and worked her farm. Alex was 14.[7]

On 24 May 1861, Alex joined the the Union Army at Quincy, Illinois. He spent the next three years and one month with the 16th Regiment of the Illinois Volunteer Infantry in Company E. He was discharged on the 24th of June 1864.[8]

He married Elizabeth in 1870 and lived in Ralls County, Missouri. She was 12 years younger than Alex.[9]

In the 1880 Census, Alex is shown living in Prairie Township of Audrain County with the first six of his eventual thirteen children.[10]

The trial was held October 8, 1896. The following men were jurors: Ed Elder, S. C. Kincaid, T. B. Hendrix, W. W. Wilson, J. T. Scott, J. T. Leeper, T. E. Rodgers, Geo. W. Green, W. M. Clanton, A. D. Bledsoe, F. P. Davis, and T. J. Holloway.

It was brought out in Willie's confession that his on-going fight with his father on Friday was because Alexander was angry with him for buying a watch in June. He thought Willie had paid too much for it. Also, Willie had worked out the first part of the year and his father had not been able to get his wages, because Willie kept them. On Friday they had fought again and his father chased him with a shotgun. While his father was gone on Saturday, he borrowed a shotgun and planned to kill him.

The Januarys had lived a long time in the Farber area. Everyone who knew Mr. January said he was a hot tempered man, who mistreated his family shamefully. He was known to have shot at his boys about a month before. Local residents felt sympathy for Willie and believed the law should be lenient.

The jury heard the evidence presented at the trial on Friday and

Saturday. At 4:10 Saturday afternoon the jury began to deliberate. At seven o'clock they returned to the court with a verdict of guilty of second degree murder. The jury set the punishment at ten years.[11]

Willie was imprisoned in the State Penitentiary at Jefferson City. In his first years he contracted tuberculosis and in 1899 he was released from prison, dying. Willie passed away soon after his release. It is believed that Willie and his father were buried in the old Farber Cemetery. A Mr. January is listed in the Farber City Cemetery as being a veteran of the Civil War. When the old cemetery was moved to make way for a parking lot, his body must have been moved. There is no stone for either father or son.

On November 11, 1896 Elizabeth applied for a widow's pension based on Alexander's military service. One factoid that was in the application was that Alexander had a disability due to his service. He was deaf from tending an artillery battery at the battle of Corinth, Mississippi. Her application number 456873 was approved and the pension of eight dollars a month began on 27 December 1897. In addition, she received two dollars a month for her six children under the age of sixteen. It was payable until they turned sixteen. At the time of her death she appeared to be living with a daughter, Mattie, in Kansas. She was dropped from the rolls on September 25, 1912.

In 1944 Kenny Segrave authored a book, Parricide in the United States 1840-1899. One of the cases studied in the book was the patricide case of William January.[12]

Endnotes

[1]The shotgun used by William was a cap and ball. With the gun loaded when an individual was ready to fire, he put a cap onto a nipple under the hammer. There could not be pressure on the cap as it would discharge, to prevent this the hammer was pulled to a half-cocked position. If you were half-cocked, you were ready for immediate action. Out of this came the phrase, don't go off half-cocked. A person with a hot temper was often half-cocked and dangerous.

[2]Mexico Weekly Ledger (Mexico, Audrain County, Missouri), 13 Aug 1896, Thursday, Vol. 38, No. 20, p. 3, cols. 2,3. Hereinafter cited as Mexico Weekly Ledger.

[3]Mexico Weekly Ledger, 13 Aug 1896.

[4]Mexico Weekly Ledger, 13 Aug 1896.

[5]Mexico Weekly Ledger, 13 Aug 1896.

[6]Mexico Weekly Ledger, 13 Aug 1896. John D. Orear was appointed Consul to Bolivia in 1913 by the President. He died in office there in 1918.

142

[7]1850 U. S. Census, Township 6 S 3 W, Pike County, Illinois; p. 121B, National Archives Roll: M432_124.

[8]1890 Veterans Schedules, District 1, Cuivre, Audrain County, Missouri; p. 2, National Archives Roll: 29.

[9]1870 U. S. Census, Jasper, Ralls County, Missouri; p. 44A, National Archives Roll: M593_802; Family History Film: 552301.

[10]1880 U. S. Census, District 3, Prairie, Audrain County, Missouri; p. 78C, National Archives Roll: 67; Family History Film: 1254672.

[11]Mexico Weekly Ledger, 15 Oct 1896, Vol. 38, No. 29, p. 1, col. 7.

[12]Kerry Segrave. Parricide in the United States 1840-1899 (Jefferson, SC: McFarland & Company, 2009).

Crumbs

Martinsburg Enterprise (Martinsburg, Audrain County, MO), 12 May 1903, Thursday, Vol. 3, No. 17, p, 1, col. 1.

ROUTE THROUGH AUDRAIN BURLINGTON CUT-OFF to PASS FINE FARMLAND BENTON CITY 3/4 MILE SOUTH

A plat of the route through Audrain county for the Burlington cut-off to Old Monroe was seen by a Ledger reporter today. The cut-off will leave the main Alton line about a mile east of the bridge over Salt River. According to the plat the new line will leave the Alton on the north side and after a few hundred yards will cross to the south. A long curve will be made and then a straight line, varying less than one degree, will be followed through the county in an east south-easterly direction. The Burlington has already bought 37 acres of land near where they leave the main line for switch yards. The following farms are named through which the road will run: R. E. Lawder, 160 acres; I. C. Sheets, 160; northeast corner of A. B. Cady's 160; E. R. Cunningham, 160; Lizzie Field, 120; passing just to the south of the Luckie farm; and barely touching the northeast corner of G. M. Gillman's 80; John E. Davis, 320 acres; Mary E. Hamilton, 160; A. D. Erisman, 160; through southwest section owned by Mrs. Lizzie Field; John Able, 90; W. E. Epperson, 130; Solomon Garver, 200; Walter Tratchel, 320; B. Waddington, 160; Elmer Johnson, 160; Mr. Town, 320; Frank Seckler, 320; M. Hoer, 240; C. Winkelman, 120; Henry Wieschhaus, 40; northeast corner of Mr. Wilburn's 40; H. Paschang, 280; northeast corner of L. Ahrens 40; H. Ahrens, 80.

Look for More Slices to come...

You might like a special slice, Bushwhacker, which is about Alvin Cobb. A taste was offered in the Little Dixie Weekender newspaper, which ran a two-part feature on him. This will be a full slice with his whole story, from his farm on the county line to Colusa, CA, and the Civil War in between.

Read an enjoyable slice about Clarence Buell. He was a drover (cowboy),personal friend of Buffalo Bill Cody (toured England with Cody's Wild West Show), long-time Martinsburger, living with his sister and nephews.

Bite into a slice relating the tale of Margaret Torreyson, pioneer school teacher. Maggie's life was devoted to education, travel, and post cards. Her home was in Martinsburg, though she taught in Vandalia and Montgomery County, including her hometown.

Find slices about Amos Ladd, founder of Laddonia; William R. Martin, founder of Martinsburg; Aaron McPike, founder of Vandalia; Harrison Glascock, who shot train robber Jim Berry; Uncle Alfred Petty, a Martinsburg fixture and a superb marksman with his Kentucky rifle; J. J. Stowe, huge landowner; the Fletcher Brothers, shot for trying to vote in Martinsburg; and C. C. Chrisman, Indian fighter, inventor, composer, business school owner, and an experimenter with chickens and fruit trees.

Perhaps you would like to suggest a slice. Tell us your favorite local story about a person, a place, or a thing. Remember each one has a history all its own.

Paul Hoer